PROPHECY
FOR TEN-TRIBE
ISRAEL

A VERSE-BY-VERSE PROPHECY STUDY

Hosea-Amos-Micah

Virtually all Scripture references are quoted from the King James translation of the Holy Bible.

Prophecy for Ten-Tribe Israel
Copyright © 2017 by Midnight Call Ministries

Published by The Olive Press, a division of Midnight Call, Inc.
West Columbia, SC 29170 U.S.A.

Copy Typists:	Lynn Jeffcoat and Kathy Roland
Copy Editor:	Kimberly Farmer
Layout/Design:	Michelle Kim
Cover Design:	Michelle Kim

Froese, Arno
    Prophecy for Ten-Tribe Israel
    ISBN #9780937422717

    1. Bible--Prophecy

Printed in the United States of America

The sole purpose of publishing this book is to encourage the readers to surrender and consecrate their lives to Christ.

All funds received from the sale of this book will be used exclusively for the furtherance of the Gospel.

No one associated with this ministry receives a royalty for any of the literature published by Midnight Call Ministries, Inc.

CONTENTS

HOSEA

Salvation

HOSEA

Book of the Bible	God's Directly Spoken Words (%)	Prophecy %*	Significant Names Listed in Each Book						
			Judah	Israel	Ephraim	Jerusalem	Zion	Heathen	Samaria
Hosea	**93.32**	**56**	**15**	**44**	**37**	**0**	**0**	**0**	**6**
Joel	57.70	68	6	3	0	6	7	5	0
Amos	80.95	58	4	30	0	2	2	1	5
Obadiah	97.69	81	1	1	1	2	2	4	1
Jonah	7.39	10	0	0	0	0	0	0	0
Micah	44.88	70	4	12	0	8	9	1	3
Nahum	40.30	74	1	1	0	0	0	0	0
Habakkuk	47.84	41	0	0	0	0	0	2	0
Zephaniah	96.92	89	3	4	0	4	2	1	0
Haggai	67.61	39	4	0	0	0	0	1	0
Zechariah	77.38	69	22	5	3	41	8	5	0
Malachi	93.80	56	3	5	0	2	0	2	0

* Percentage of book as prophecy according to *Tim LaHaye Prophecy Study Bible*

13

Introduction to the Book of Hosea

The book of Hosea is the first in line of the popularly called 12 Minor Prophets. Why Minor? Mainly due to the short content of these books, but the message is no less important than other prophets such as Isaiah or Jeremiah.

Since the prophet Hosea hails from the Northern Kingdom, his message is primarily directed to the ten-tribe rebellious Israel.

It is noteworthy to mention that virtually the entire book of Hosea consists of the directly spoken words of God.

We may divide Hosea's writings into two parts; in the first three chapters, Israel's Unfaithfulness, Israel's Rejection, and Israel's Reacceptance are revealed. Chapters 4—14 expose the sin and punishment in view of Israel's past, present, and future.

According to the *Tim LaHaye Prophecy Study Bible*, 56 percent of the content of the book of Hosea is prophecy.

As we study this first book of the Minor Prophets, we need to take note of the three particular groups: 1) Israel, meaning the ten-tribe rebellious Israel; 2) the kingdom of Judah, also called Israel; and 3) the Gentiles, highlighted in particular through the kingdom of Nineveh.

The prime target of Hosea is the ten-tribe rebellious Israel, climaxing in the words, "I will no more have mercy upon the house of Israel...ye are not my people." Nevertheless, there is a remnant, as expressed in the last chapter, "I will heal their backsliding, I will love them freely: for mine anger is turned away from him" (Hosea 14:4).

Chapter 1

Introduction

The ten-tribe, rebellious kingdom of Israel has no future because the Lord "will cause to cease the kingdom of the house of Israel." That means the independent identity of the ten-tribe kingdom will no longer exist. This is vividly expressed by the name of Hosea's first son, Jezreel, indicating judgment upon the house of Jehu. It spells the end of Israel's military power.

Next comes a daughter, Loruhamah, meaning "not having obtained mercy." Finally, a son, Loammi, confirming the utter end of the independent, ten-tribe rebellious Israel with the words, "Ye are not my people."

God's Command to Hosea

Hosea 1:1: "The word of the LORD that came unto Hosea, the son of Beeri, in the days of Uzziah, Jotham, Ahaz, and Hezekiah, kings of Judah, and in the days of Jeroboam the son of Joash, king of Israel."

(See) 2 Peter 1:21

In English, we may translate the name "Hosea" with the word "help" or "salvation." The first three chapters in particular demonstrate Israel's unfaithfulness, clearly pictured in Hosea's marriage to adulterous Gomer, the daughter of Diblaim.

15

Something unusual is written in verse 2:

> **Hosea 1:2:** "The beginning of the word of the LORD by Hosea. And the LORD said to Hosea, Go, take unto thee a wife of whoredoms and children of whoredoms: for the land hath committed great whoredom, departing from the LORD."

(See) Deuteronomy 31:16; Judges 2:17; Psalm 78:27

This is strange because Hosea does not protest; he does as told. That's one thing. The other is that God, through Moses, had strictly forbidden such a union. Quite apparently, Hosea was fully committed to the direct command of God, who said, "Go, take unto thee a wife of whoredoms." He followed this command because he was an obedient child of God; he did what he was told.

Go, Come, Do

Incidentally "go, come, and do" are the three most important words for parents to take note of when raising their children. If these three fundamentals are not taught to my child by the time he can understand them, then I venture to say I have failed in his upbringing. Lately, everybody seems to blame others instead of self: the liberal school, temptation, corruption, the teachers, bad company, etc.

Let's look at an example in the New Testament in Matthew 8:9. Here a Roman centurion testifies: "I am a man under authority, having soldiers under me: and I say to this man, Go, and he goeth; and to another, Come,

16

and he cometh; and to my servant, Do this, and he doeth it." Note that this Roman military man confesses first of all that he is under authority. That means he was obedient, which resulted in him having authority over others; in this case, soldiers. Go, come and do. Our own obedience results in obedience by others. It is extremely difficult if I am disobedient to God or to man, to exercise authority over my children.

Hosea reacted immediately:

Hosea 1:3: "So he went and took Gomer the daughter of Diblaim; which conceived, and bare him a son."

That marriage resulted in a son, and the Lord Himself chooses the name:

Hosea 1:4: "And the LORD said unto him, Call his name Jezreel; for yet a little while, and I will avenge the blood of Jezreel upon the house of Jehu, and will cause to cease the kingdom of the house of Israel."

House of Israel

We must place the definition "house of Israel" in its proper context. Jehu was king of the ten-tribe house of Israel. So, the primary target of the message is the Northern Kingdom.

However, Judah is also the "house of Israel." Daniel, for example, was identified as one of "the children of Israel" (Daniel 1:3). When Daniel confesses the sins of his people, he says, "Yea, all Israel have transgressed thy law" (Daniel 9:11). Or in verse 20: "...Whiles I was

17

PROPHECY FOR TEN-TRIBE ISRAEL

speaking, and praying, and confessing my sin and the sin of my people Israel...."

Later in history, on the day of Pentecost, we hear the Apostle Peter state: "Ye men of Israel...let all the house of Israel know assuredly" (Acts 2:22, 36). Then he says again, "Ye men of Israel...to all the people of Israel..." (3:12; 4:10). But he was addressing Judah, the Jews in Jerusalem. Subsequently, both Judah and Israel are the "house of Israel."

However, it is important to show the separation between Israel/Judah and ten-tribe Israel. If we don't, then we fall for the deception proclaimed within Churchianity, that Israel has been permanently rejected. Many say, Israel has no more spiritual significance; they are out of the picture. But according to Scripture, that's not the case. Only the ten-tribe, rebellious kingdom of Israel came under total judgment.

Hosea 1:5: "And it shall come to pass at that day, that I will break the bow of Israel in the valley of Jezreel."

This is the end of the political power structure of ten-tribe Israel, as a separate identity from Judah.

Loruhamah
Next, Hosea's wife gives birth to a daughter:

Hosea 1:6: "And she conceived again, and bare a daughter. And God said unto him, Call her name Loruhamah: for I will no more have mercy upon the house of Israel; but I will utterly take them away."

This name Loruhamah has a message, "not under grace...no mercy...not having obtained mercy." The children of Hosea, by his adulterous wife Gomer, picture God's judgment upon ten-tribe Israel: "I will utterly take them away."

Judah-Israel

Although some commentators would disagree, I do like to point to the next verse, showing the distinct difference between the ten-tribe house of Israel and the house of Judah:

Hosea 1:7: "But I will have mercy upon the house of Judah, and will save them by the LORD their God, and will not save them by bow, nor by sword, nor by battle, by horses, nor by horsemen."

Note that God's mercy over Judah is not due to political or military achievement; it will purely be grace: "not... by bow, nor by sword, nor by battle, by horses, nor by horsemen." This means the entire military force will not participate in nor contribute to God's act of mercy.

If the Jews would have taken note of such prophecies, they would not have rebelled against Babylon, against the Persians, the Greeks or the Romans. Neither would there have been the Judah Maccabee revolt or the tragedy of Masada.

Waiting for the Promised One

Israel will have to wait. What are they waiting for? For the revelation of the Promised One, the Messiah of Israel.

This waiting is the strength of the Jews.

I am reading a Jewish book, copyright 1929, in which the author, Ludwig Stern, writes: "I confirm with perfect honesty the absolute assurance that I am waiting for the coming of the Messiah. Though He may delay long, I shall patiently wait for Him daily until He comes."

That is what many of us Bible believers call the imminency of the Lord's return. We are not waiting for certain days, dates or Jewish holidays, nor are we waiting for signs and wonders. We are waiting for the coming of Jesus in the clouds of heaven. It is the Lord Himself who admonished us: "Therefore be ye also ready: for in such an hour as ye think not the Son of man cometh" (Matthew 24:44).

Loammi

Another child is born:

Hosea 1:8-9: "Now when she had weaned Loruhamah, she conceived, and bare a son. 9 Then said God, Call his name Loammi: for ye are not my people, and I will not be your God."

The third child too is named by God Himself: Loammi, meaning "not my people." Again, this reconfirms God's rejection of ten-tribe Israel as a separate identity. But immediately after this devastating prophecy, we read an amazing statement of hope and salvation:

Hosea 1:10: "Yet the number of the children of Israel shall

20

be as the sand of the sea, which cannot be measured nor numbered; and it shall come to pass, that in the place where it was said unto them, Ye are not my people, there it shall be said unto them, Ye are the sons of the living God."

(See) Genesis 26:4; Exodus 32:13; Numbers 23:10; Deuteronomy 1:10; 1 Kings 3:8; 1 Chronicles 27:23; John 1:12; Romans 9:27

Israel: God's Chosen

This again should confirm our belief that the people of Israel collectively—Israel-Judah and the remnant of the ten-tribe Israel—are still "the sons of the living God."

Quite obviously, there is no outward evidence of such at this moment. Much good, but equally much evil, can be said about the Jews and Israel today. Yet that does not change God's eternal resolutions. We must not make the mistake of limiting the fulfillment of prophecy to our own time and terms. God has no problem with time: a thousand years are for Him as one day, and one day as a thousand years.

That statement also devastates all of our configuration and mathematical theories. When you make a thousand years one day, and vice versa, that's when you stop figuring; you just give up! It goes far beyond any reasonable intellectual calculations.

Israel's existence is actually based on the existence of the universe, as evidenced in Jeremiah 31:35-36: "Thus saith the LORD, which giveth the sun for a light by day, and the ordinances of the moon and of the stars for a light by night, which divideth the sea when the waves thereof roar; The LORD of hosts is his name: If those ordinances depart from before me, saith the LORD, then the seed of Israel also shall cease from being a nation before me for ever." Although Israel ceased to be a nation as a geopolitical identity—it was not visible on a map for over 2,000 years—from God's perspective, Israel never ceased to be a nation—and never will.

Reunion

Hosea 1:11: "Then shall the children of Judah and the children of Israel be gathered together, and appoint themselves one head, and they shall come up out of the land: for great shall be the day of Jezreel."

Here we see the gathering of the remnant of the children of Israel to the tribe of Judah. Today's Jews do not identify themselves by different tribes; they all are Jews, and that points to Judah.

The Lord will save Judah with the remnant of the ten-tribe Israel, and He will do it based on His grace, as we have seen in verse 7.

Then they shall "appoint themselves one head." We know who that "one head" is: He is the One they shall mourn for, as documented in Zechariah 12:10: "And I will pour upon the house of David, and upon the inhabitants of Jerusalem, the spirit of grace and of supplications: and they shall look upon me whom they have pierced, and they shall mourn for him, as one mourneth for his only son, and shall be in bitterness for him, as one that is in bitterness for his firstborn."

22

The remnant of ten-tribe rebellious Israel, united with the royal tribe Judah, will recognize the Messiah.

This, incidentally, is the message throughout the prophets: Israel's election, their sin and rejection, and their reacceptance based on the grace of God.

We do not know what next year will be like; we do not know the future, but we know the One who holds the future in His hands. Blessed is he who keeps his spiritual ears tuned to the precious, holy Word of God. Such a one will not be ashamed at His coming.

Chapter 2

Introduction

This chapter exposes how Israel broke God's covenant by their practice of idolatry. The twenty-three verses of chapter 2 consist entirely of God's speaking. Irrevocable judgment is proclaimed, but at the same time, God's acts of unmeasurable grace, guaranteeing restoration.

Israel Obtains Mercy

Hosea 2:1: "Say ye unto your brethren, Ammi; and to your sisters, Ruhamah."

Note the difference. In chapter 1, verse 9, the son was called Loammi, meaning "not my people," but here he is called Ammi, meaning "my people." The same goes for Loruhamah (verse 6), meaning "not having obtained mercy," to Ruhamah, "having obtained mercy." The children of this sinful and unfaithful woman are the ones who will experience the unspeakable grace of God, an act of mercy no one would have thought possible.

Children Plead for Mother

Hosea 2:2-5: "Plead with your mother, plead: for she is not my wife, neither am I her husband: let her therefore put away her whoredoms out of her sight, and her adulteries from between her breasts; 3 Lest I strip her naked, and set her as in the day that she was born, and make her as a wilderness, and set her like a dry land, and slay her with thirst. 4 And I will not have mercy upon her children; for they be the children of whoredoms. 5 For their mother hath played the harlot: she that conceived them hath done shamefully: for she said, I will go after my lovers, that give me my bread and my water, my wool and my flax, mine oil and my drink."

(See) Isaiah 50:1; Jeremiah 3:1, 9, 13; 13:22; 44:17; Ezekiel 16:25; 19:13; Amos 8:11

This is rather strange: the children are pointing out the sins of their mother. But this prophetic utterance is not limited to Gomer, the mother of Ammi and Ruhamah, but includes all of Israel. This is evident from verse 15, where it says, "as in the day when she came up out of the land of Egypt." It is speaking about the nation of Israel collectively.

Horrendous Judgment

The Bible reports of the horrendous judgment Israel had to go through as a nation. What was spoken by Moses the prophet became a painful reality for the people throughout the millennia.

When God says, "Lest I strip her naked...and slay her with thirst...And I will not have mercy upon her children," then we need only search the annals of history to find out that it came true. Israel faced total eradication from the face of the earth many times throughout their 2,600 year dispersion.

Destruction in Place of Peace

In recent history, we saw Israel's hope awakened when two men of Jewish roots, Karl Marx and Friedrich Engels, published the *Communist Manifesto* in 1848. It was supposed to give equality to the Jews and pave the way for Jews to be integrated into the respective host nation. We know how it turned out. Instead of liberty, they experienced bondage. For approximately 70 years, the Soviet Union made it extremely difficult for Jews to openly practice their Judaism. Neither could they migrate to Israel—the land of their fathers.

At the very beginning of the Nazi Empire, a number of Jews enthusiastically supported this nationalistic system, but it turned out to be the greatest catastrophe the Jews have ever experienced. Over six million souls perished in the diabolically designed death factories of the Nazi Empire.

Hosea 2:6-7: "Therefore, behold, I will hedge up thy way with thorns, and make a wall, that she shall not find her paths. 7 And she shall follow after her lovers, but she shall not overtake them; and she shall seek them, but shall not find them: then shall she say, I will go and return to my first husband; for then was it better with me than now."

(See) Job 19:8; Ezekiel 16:8; Luke 15:18

Israel came to a dead end often; there were many "hedges" and "walls" in their path, and the return was also made impossible. Israel's situation was all but hopeless.

God the Provider

Next, the Word of God confirms an apparently hidden truth; namely, that God was the Provider throughout the ages.

Hosea 2:8-9: "For she did not know that I gave her corn, and wine, and oil, and multiplied her silver and gold, which they prepared for Baal. 9 Therefore will I return, and take away my corn in the time thereof, and my wine in the season thereof, and will recover my wool and my flax given to cover her nakedness."

There is much evidence in Scripture that the Israelites had convinced themselves they were righteous people, deserving the blessing of the Lord. They did not realize that what they had was due to the grace of God. This is expressed with the words, "I gave her...my corn...my wine...my wool...my flax...."

Catastrophe Follows

Hosea 2:10-13: "And now will I discover her lewdness in the sight of her lovers, and none shall deliver her out of mine hand. 11 I will also cause all her mirth to cease, her feast days, her new moons, and her sabbaths, and all her solemn feasts. 12 And I will destroy her vines and her fig trees, whereof she hath said, These are my rewards that my lovers have given me: and I will make them a forest, and the beasts of the field shall eat them. 13 And I will visit upon her the days of Baalim, wherein she burned incense to them, and she decked herself with her earrings and her jewels, and she went after her lovers, and forgat me, saith the LORD."

(See) Judges 3:7; Isaiah 5:5; 24:7; Jeremiah 7:34; Ezekiel 23:40; Amos 8:10

What a horrendous catastrophe. Many judgments had befallen the Jewish people in the lands of their captivity. Only a remnant escaped Hitler's gas ovens, and later from behind the Iron Curtain. The Jews literally came to their land empty-handed, with just the clothes on their back. When they arrived, often at the risk of their lives, they found that the land of Israel was indeed a barren wilderness.

Grace Follows Judgment

Hosea 2:14: "Therefore, behold, I will allure her, and bring her into the wilderness, and speak comfortably unto her."

(See) Ezekiel 20:35

What an unspeakable act of grace! This verse almost seems like it doesn't belong here, like it comes out of another chapter, even another book. The Lord had just spoken in a very penetrating and exposing manner, uncovering the horrible sins of His people Israel, but then suddenly turns around and begins to say, "Therefore...I will...speak comfortably unto her."

It is quite interesting that God does not speak to His people directly, but first says, "I will...bring her into the wilderness...."

This, of course, reminds us that Israel was brought out of Egypt, away from the idol-worshiping people and into the wilderness, where indeed God spoke with His people when He appeared on Mount Sinai. Later, Moses recalls this event: "Did ever people hear the voice of God speaking out of the midst of the fire, as thou hast heard, and live?" (Deuteronomy 4:33).

We may also assume that "the wilderness" is an allegory of the isolation aspect of Israel among the nations. But it had and has a purpose: God is speaking "comfortably unto her."

Zionism—the fuel powering the Jews to return to Israel—is officially credited to the father of modern Zionism, Theodor Herzl, but we know that above and beyond any initiative by anyone, the return is authorized by God Himself.

More Grace

To help us in our search for a more applicable answer, let us read the next verse:

Hosea 2:15: "And I will give her her vineyards from thence, and the valley of Achor for a door of hope: and she shall sing there, as in the days of her youth, and as in the day when she came up out of the land of Egypt."

(See) Joshua 7:26; Isaiah 65:10

This doubtless is the restoration of the land of Israel, which is symbolized by the joy of agricultural products,

29

particularly the vineyards.

Also, the spiritual restoration of Israel is guaranteed: "she shall sing." That means there will be rejoicing in the Lord, which can only be done when they recognize Him.

God Prepares a Safe Place

From Revelation 12, we learn that God has prepared a special place for the children of Israel in the wilderness: "And the woman fled into the wilderness, where she hath a place prepared of God, that they should feed her there a thousand two hundred and threescore days...And to the woman were given two wings of a great eagle, that she might fly into the wilderness, into her place, where she is nourished for a time, and times, and half a time, from the face of the serpent" (Revelation 12:6, 14). This woman is Israel. She brought forth the man child, destined "to rule all nations with a rod of iron" (verse 5). We must emphasize the last sentence, revealing the identity of the King of Israel and the Son of God, Jesus Christ: "...and her child was caught up unto God, and to his throne."

Is Petra the Place?

There are a number of theories regarding the place in the wilderness. Most of my colleagues have determined that it is a place in Jordan in the mountains of Petra. Having been to this place, I consider it a 100% death trap because there is no way out once you are in Petra. There is virtually no water, electricity, sewage system, or proper healthcare facilities. Israel would be at the mercy of the enemies, who could easily destroy the entire nation with just a few bombs.

When things are not easily and plainly understood intellectually, then we must go back to Scripture. What does Scripture say? "A place prepared of God." Therefore, instead of coming to the conclusion that this is Petra, where the Jews will live in caves under primitive conditions, I believe when the Lord prepares something for His people, He will prepare a "five star hotel" with all the luxuries for a modern nation to exist and to function in this "wilderness."

Supernatural Escape

How will the Jews get to this safe place? Here the Bible gives the answer, "To the woman were give two wings of a great eagle, that she might fly into the wilderness, into her place." If we take this literally, then we must assume it will be an aerial evacuation to a certain place. Scripture reads: "two wings of a great eagle." If you ask me what they are, I confess, I don't know. But it's all sufficient for me to understand that God is going to intervene supernaturally; He will take His people to safety for 3 ½ years, in a place that He has prepared for them. I think it is a mistake to explain everything in physical and geographical terms.

An example: When Israel walked through the desert for 40 years, God intervened supernaturally. Moses testified to that fact in Deuteronomy 29:5: "And I have led you forty years in the wilderness: your clothes are not waxen old upon you, and thy shoe is not waxen old upon thy foot." That is intellectually incomprehensible;

clothes wear out, and so do shoes. Thus, we see God's supernatural interference.

The Cleansing Process

Hosea 2:16-17: "And it shall be at that day, saith the LORD, that thou shalt call me Ishi; and shalt call me no more Baali. 17 For I will take away the names of Baalim out of her mouth, and they shall no more be remembered by their name."

(See) Exodus 23:13

Here we see God's blood covenant being made effective for Israel. It's not the covenant based on the blood of bulls and goats, which cannot take away sins, but it is the blood of the Son, the Lord Jesus Christ. That is the foundation on which He reestablishes His intimate relationship. Israel will no longer be connected to *Baali,* which means "my Lord," but she shall call Him *Ishi,* that is, "my husband."

An All-Inclusive Restoration

Hosea 2:18: "And in that day will I make a covenant for them with the beasts of the field, and with the fowls of heaven, and with the creeping things of the ground: and I will break the bow and the sword and the battle out of the earth, and will make them to lie down safely."

(See) Leviticus 26:5; Job 5:23; Isaiah 2:4; 11:6; Jeremiah 23:6; Zechariah 9:10

It is moving to read the words "I will" or "will I" no less than 23 times in chapter 2. God promises restoration of the animal world and the abolishment of weapons in Israel and the world.

War Will Cease

The desire of Israel, and for that matter all the people of the world, will finally come. Every nation on the face of the earth desires peace. But each nation, under the rulership of Lucifer, the god of this world, thinks that only they are right and everybody else is wrong; subsequently, they want to enforce their rights and their understanding of peace upon other nations. Thus, we have war. But war will cease when Jesus comes and establishes His kingdom of peace on earth. The military will cease to exist: "I will break the bow and the sword and the battle out of the earth." That will take place at the implementation of the millennium of peace.

How will it be accomplished? Micah 4:3 gives the answer: "And he shall judge among many people, and rebuke strong nations afar off; and they shall beat their swords into plowshares, and their spears into pruninghooks: nation shall not lift up a sword against nation, neither shall they learn war any more." He will judge the nations; He will institute true righteousness; He will eliminate all military forces in the world; He will implement true peace.

Deeper Relationship Announced

Hosea 2:19-20: "And I will betroth thee unto me for ever; yea, I will betroth thee unto me in righteousness, and in judgment, and in lovingkindness, and in mercies. 20 I will even betroth thee unto me in faithfulness: and thou shalt know the LORD."

(See) Isaiah 54:13; Jeremiah 31:33

This reveals how God desires a personal, intimate relationship with His people. It is none other than amazing grace, unspeakable pardon and immeasurable love for His people.

"I Will Hear"

Hosea 2:21-22: "And it shall come to pass in that day, I will hear, saith the LORD, I will hear the heavens, and they shall hear the earth; 22 And the earth shall hear the corn, and the wine, and the oil; and they shall hear Jezreel."

(See) Zechariah 8:12

Note the word "hear." In Hebrew it is *aw-naw*, to "pay attention." This is not the same as "Hear the word of the Lord" in chapter 4:1, where the people are admonished to "hear."

The result for the land will be "Jezreel," that is, "God sows." He will cause the land to bring forth abundantly.

Next comes the threefold "I will" of God Almighty:

> **Hosea 2:23:** "And I will sow her unto me in the earth; and I will have mercy upon her that had not obtained mercy; and I will say to them which were not my people, Thou art my people; and they shall say, Thou art my God."

(See) Zechariah 10:9; 13:9

A Personal Message

The second chapter of the book of Hosea has an important message for each one of us: regardless of our shortcoming, failures, and transgressions, the grace of God is available to each individually. It may well be that He has led you into the "wilderness"; that means separated from all your goals, plans for the future, all you had hoped for. Now there is nothing left but you, "the wilderness" and God. Thus, the time has come for you to do as Israel will do, "call [Him] Ishi," "my husband."

It is the Apostle Paul who expressed his deep desire for the Church in 2 Corinthians 11:2: "For I am jealous over you with godly jealousy: for I have espoused you to one husband, that I may present you as a chaste virgin to Christ."

Chapter 3

Introduction

This chapter guarantees Israel's continuing existence. Even without a political and religious identity, Israel will remain Israel, but never independent of Judah. This is highlighted by God's command to Hosea to love an adulterous woman.

God gives His prophet instruction and does not leave out any details. We read somewhat repeated statements regarding Israel's unfaithfulness, their transgression against God's commandment, and God's punishment by various means such as natural catastrophes and enemies. Yet over and again God's grace breaks through. The end result will be, "Thou art my people; and they shall say, Thou art my God."

Another Woman?

In verse 1, we read of a commandment of the Lord regarding an adulterous woman:

Hosea 3:1: "Then said the LORD unto me, Go yet, love a woman beloved of her friend, yet an adulteress, according to the love of the LORD toward the children of Israel, who look to other gods, and love flagons of wine."

Many scholars believe it is the same woman, Gomer, who is named in chapter 1, verse 3. However, there is no mention of her name; it does not say the "same woman" or "your wife," but simply "a woman."

Important to understand is that God in a very practical way demonstrates His deep love for His people Israel on the one hand, and exposes the horrible wickedness and unfaithfulness of Israel on the other.

Fifteen Pieces of Silver

Hosea 3:2: "So I bought her to me for fifteen pieces of silver, and for an homer of barley, and an half homer of barley:"

This harlot-wife is bought for money, fifteen pieces of silver. This seems prophetic because fifteen represents rest. Hosea is paying her to rest, to stop committing adultery.

Sustenance is provided, one and a half homer of barley. That's more than the weight which would normally be carried by a donkey. Barley was relatively plentiful during biblical times. It was the grain for bread for the poor people. With this demonstration, God was telling Israel that they will be put on hold, but provision will be made.

Faithfulness by Order

Hosea 3:3: "And I said unto her, Thou shalt abide for me many days; thou shalt not play the harlot, and thou shalt not be for another man: so will I also be for thee."

(See) Deuteronomy 21:13

God is showing us Israel's future. We know, for example, that after the return from Babylonian captivity, Israel had separated herself from idol worship. Archaeology reveals that after the destruction of the temple in Jerusalem, idol worship among Jews could rarely be found. An abundance of literature as well as ancient Jewish synagogues testify to the fact that pagan idolatry was mostly absent from the Jews.

The Missing Timespan

Now comes an important prophecy:

Hosea 3:4: "For the children of Israel shall abide many days without a king, and without a prince, and without a sacrifice, and without an image, and without an ephod, and without teraphim:"

(See) Exodus 28:6

How long are these "many days"? Daniel's prophecy gives us a clue: "After threescore and two weeks shall Messiah be cut off, but not for himself" (Daniel 9:26). The Hebrew translation is helpful: "After those 62 weeks, the anointed one will disappear and vanish." The German Menge translation puts it this way: "After 62 year weeks, the anointed shall lose his life, but without judgment." Schlachter reads: "After 62 weeks, the anointed shall be eliminated and there shall be nothing more." Reading the various translations, one immediately realizes the difficulty in finding the right words. Yet the message is clear: the anointed is Jesus; the time span,

62 weeks, is clearly given. He is unjustly killed, and then follows nothing for an unspecified time, or "many days."

Israel Stands Still

Politically speaking, "without a king" and "without a prince" means no nation. Religiously, "without a sacrifice...without an image...without an ephod...without teraphim" means no temple; no more biblically-ordained sacrifice and priestly service. That certainly has come true for the last 2,000 years. Israel had no political leader, and they were forbidden by law to offer sacrifices because there was no temple, nor were there the necessary utensils and the priestly attire to execute the sacrifice. In this case, we may identify the "many days" as 2,000-plus years. In plain words, the Jews lost their political, geographical, and religious identity—but they kept the Word, the Bible.

Israel's Return

Although Israel supposedly liberated Jerusalem from foreign occupation on 7 June 1967, the Jews still do not have the authority to do with Jerusalem as they please. The whole world would act immediately if Israel were to build their temple on Mt. Moriah. It's simply out of the question at this time.

But then comes the promise of Israel's return:

Hosea 3:5: "Afterward shall the children of Israel return, and seek the LORD their God, and David their king; and shall fear the LORD and his goodness in the latter days."

(See) 1 Kings 12:16; Isaiah 27:12-13; 55:3-4; Jeremiah 3:22-23; 30:9;
Micah 4:1

Some may now say that Israel's return to the land of their fathers in recent decades, does not qualify as the fulfillment of this prophecy, because the motive of their return was not to "seek the Lord their God." That is true; the Jews' return to the land of Israel was strictly motivated by their desire to exist, to be independent, to be secure. They had just experienced the greatest tragedy in all of Jewish history, namely the Holocaust, where over 6 million Jews perished due to Hitler's diabolically devised plan to exterminate all Jews.

There is an abundance of documentation available that describes in detail the return of the Jews to the land of Israel. But, as already mentioned, the prime motive was not to "seek the Lord their God."

Communist Philosophy

Actually, Israel's return to the Promised Land was motivated by communist philosophy. Communist doctrine insists on five elementary rights of civilized people, according to Karl Marx: food, shelter, clothing, education and healthcare.

It is rather ironic that Israel's founding fathers were strongly influenced by communism and not the Bible. Virtually all of their leaders were communist-educated. Actually, it served Israel well in the beginning. They established communes called Kibbutzim. Everybody shared everything equally, whether a trench digger, a doctor, or an intellectual with a PhD. Thus, the beginning of the famous Kibbutz movement was patterned after communism. This system guaranteed Israel's sustenance as a nation. Food is and was essential, and the Kibbutz was the provider.

Founding the State of Israel

During one of our conferences in the early 70s, Professor Pinhas Lapedi stated: "A country can exist without politicians, even without schools and bankers, but it cannot exist without farmers. People must eat to stay alive."

When the nation was proclaimed on 14 May 1948, no one came to help. As a matter of fact, Britain and the United States had an arms embargo in place. Only communist Czechoslovakia was willing to sell Second World War weapons to the Jews, all under the umbrella of the Soviet Union. The equipment for Israel's meager air force came packaged in crates by ship, and some in planes by air from the communist Soviet Union.

Fulfillment Yet to Come

This should suffice to show that they were not seeking the Lord. Nevertheless, between when "the children of Israel return" and they "seek the Lord their God," some time will transpire. We make a mistake when we think that this all happens at the moment of their return.

First, they will return. That has been in process now, day after day, year after year. The second part, the seeking of the Lord, is still to come. Israel knows the invitation of the prophet Isaiah: "Incline your ear, and come unto me: hear, and your soul shall live; and I will make an everlasting covenant with you, even the sure mercies of David" (Isaiah 55:3). What will be the end thereof? Israel "shall fear the Lord and his goodness in the latter days." That is yet to come!

Chapter 4

Introduction

Chapter 4 is sometimes headlined, "Pronunciation of Judgment." That is very fitting. The prophet exposes Israel's sinful behavior, particularly emphasizing the failure of the priesthood. That leads to the absence of truth, mercy and real knowledge of God.

Thus, he exposes the entire nation as violators of God's law.

Controversy

Hosea 4:1: "Hear the word of the LORD, ye children of Israel: for the LORD hath a controversy with the inhabitants of the land, because there is no truth, nor mercy, nor knowledge of God in the land."

(See) Jeremiah 4:22; Micah 6:2

The word "controversy" stands out in this verse. What does it mean? The answer is found in 1 Timothy 3:16: "And without controversy great is the mystery of godliness: God was manifest in the flesh, justified in the Spirit, seen of angels, preached unto the Gentiles, believed on in the world, received up into glory." This is the answer to the great controversy: God manifested in the flesh. That is how God settled the controversy between His holiness and man's sinfulness.

Why didn't He simply destroy mankind and hand us over to the prince of darkness? John 3:16 answers: "For God so loved the world, that he gave his only begotten Son, that whosoever believeth in him should not perish, but have everlasting life."

That's how God solved the controversy with a lost humanity. Here, however, the controversy is with Israel—"the inhabitants of the land."

Israel's Total Failure

When we read the fourth chapter of Hosea, we realize that God was not asking Israel to repent, but He was making an arbitrary statement of their lost condition: "there is no truth, nor mercy, nor knowledge of God in the land." The text does not say, "the lack thereof," or that the majority of the Israelis had failed, but this verse is describing the entire nation.

While God is addressing Israel, particularly the ten-tribe Israel, Judah was not excluded, as we will see later.

Prophecy for the Church

This warning also relates to the Church today, based on 2 Timothy 3:16: "All scripture is given by inspiration of God, and is profitable for doctrine, for reproof, for correction, for instruction in righteousness." We must keep in mind that the Church of Jesus Christ has a Jewish foundation, "built upon the foundation of the apostles and prophets, Jesus Christ himself being the chief corner stone" (Ephesians 2:20). This reveals the Church's interdependence with Israel.

In 1 Corinthians 10, the apostle specifically stresses

that we should take heed both of the positive and also the negative history of the children of Israel: "And were all baptized unto Moses in the cloud and in the sea; And did all eat the same spiritual meat; And did all drink the same spiritual drink: for they drank of that spiritual Rock that followed them: and that Rock was Christ" (verses 2-4). Thus, we see the organic unity between Israel and the Church.

Furthermore, the apostle exposes the sins of Israel in order to warn the Church:

"Neither be ye idolaters, as were some of them; as it is written, The people sat down to eat and drink, and rose up to play. Neither let us commit fornication, as some of them committed, and fell in one day three and twenty thousand. Neither let us tempt Christ, as some of them also tempted, and were destroyed of serpents. Neither murmur ye, as some of them also murmured, and were destroyed of the destroyer" (verses 7-10).

We are to take careful notice of this event, because verse 11 says: "Now all these things happened unto them for examples: and they are written for our admonition, upon whom the ends of the world are come."

Often, we are guilty of dissecting the Bible to fit our own understanding, and not allowing the Holy Spirit to guide us into all truth.

Prophecy Past, Present and Future

Hosea 4:2-3: "By swearing, and lying, and killing, and stealing, and committing adultery, they break out, and blood toucheth blood. 3 Therefore shall the land mourn, and every one that dwelleth therein shall languish, with the beasts of the field, and with the fowls of heaven; yea, the fishes of the sea also shall be taken away."

This reveals total disregard for God's law. Subsequently, the land also suffers. Note, however, that this prophecy reaches far into the future; this suffering will not only affect the beast in the field, the fowl in the air, but also the fish in the sea.

The land suffered after Israel was expelled from her territory. This affected the beasts in the field and the birds in the air, but not the fish. Therefore, we must assume that this pronunciation of prophecy reaches directly into the time of the Great Tribulation, when a third of the sea will turn to blood. As a result, we read: "And the third part of the creatures which were in the sea, and had life, died; and the third part of the ships were destroyed" (Revelation 8:9).

The Failed Priesthood

Next we see the hearts of the people remained unaffected by all of God's judgments. Even the priests had become insensitive to God's Word.

Hosea 4:4-5: "Yet let no man strive, nor reprove another: for thy people are as they that strive with the priest. 5 Therefore shalt thou fall in the day, and the prophet also shall fall with thee in the night, and I will destroy thy mother."

(See) Isaiah 5:13; Jeremiah 6:4

The priests were segregated from the public; they were set apart, sanctified for the Lord's service. But that special position had also been lost. Worse yet, the phrase, "I will destroy thy mother" means there will be no descendants. Take the mothers away and there won't be a next generation.

Failed Knowledge

Hosea 4:6: "My people are destroyed for lack of knowledge: because thou hast rejected knowledge, I will also reject thee, that thou shalt be no priest to me: seeing thou hast forgotten the law of thy God, I will also forget thy children."

Spiritually, this verse applies to the Church as well, because there is a lack of knowledge regarding the Word of God among Christians today. This reminds us of the words of Jesus, "Without me ye can do nothing." If we don't hold to the Head, then our service, dedication, even our sacrifice, will be in vain.

From Glory to Shame

Hosea 4:7-11: "As they were increased, so they sinned against me: therefore will I change their glory into shame. 8 They eat up the sin of my people, and they set their heart on their iniquity. 9 And there shall be, like people, like priest: and I will punish them for their ways, and reward them their doings. 10 For they shall eat, and not have enough: they shall commit whoredom, and shall not increase: because they have left off to take heed to the LORD. 11 Whoredom and wine and new wine take away the heart."

We know that Israel is destined to become the glory of all nations, a light unto the Gentiles; however, here we see that instead of glory shame is demonstrated.

Although modern Israel has made many great advances in science and technology, the Jews remain segregated. The nations of the world still treat Israel differently. Israel cannot do what other nations take for granted; for example, "To the victor belongs the spoil." By now, Israel should have taken possession of all of the Promised Land, but the nations of the world will not allow it.

This desire is evident in the Church as well. The general attitude is, "How close to the world can I get and still be a Christian?" instead of, "How far away from the world can I get to draw closer to Jesus?"

Israel's Idolatry
Not only had Israel forsaken the law and forgotten His instruction, but now they indulge in full-fledged idolatry:

Hosea 4:12-14: "My people ask counsel at their stocks, and their staff declareth unto them: for the spirit of whoredoms hath caused them to err, and they have gone a whoring from under their God. 13 They sacrifice upon the tops of the mountains, and burn incense upon the hills, under oaks and poplars and elms, because the shadow thereof is good: therefore your daughters shall commit whoredom, and your spouses shall commit adultery. 14 I will not punish your daughters when they commit whoredom, nor your spouses when they commit adultery: for themselves are separated with whores, and they sacrifice with harlots: therefore the people that doth not understand shall fall."

(See) Job 31:9-10; Isaiah 44:20; Jeremiah 2:27; Amos 7:17; Romans 1:28;
Revelation 17:2

God gave up His people. This again confirms that the ten-tribe Israel was on the way to being annihilated. However, their prophet makes a distinction between the ten-tribe Israel and Judah:

Hosea 4:15: "Though thou, Israel, play the harlot, yet let not Judah offend; and come not ye unto Gilgal, neither go ye up to Bethaven, nor swear, The LORD liveth."

(See) Amos 4:4; 8:14

Judah is warned not to participate in Israel's idolatry. In the end, however, Judah failed too. Nevertheless, God's promise did not depart from Judah. In the last book of the Bible, we read, "...behold, the Lion of the tribe of Judah, the Root of David, hath prevailed to open the book, and to loose the seven seals thereof" (Revelation 5:5).

The chapter concludes with these words:

Hosea 4:16-19: "For Israel slideth back as a backsliding heifer: now the LORD will feed them as a lamb in a large place. 17 Ephraim is joined to idols: let him alone. 18 Their drink is sour: they have committed whoredom continually: her rulers with shame do love, Give ye. 19 The wind hath bound her up in her wings, and they shall be ashamed because of their sacrifices."

(See) Matthew 15:14

The ten-tribe Israel does not have a future as an independent identity; God gave them up. This reminds us of Revelation 22:11: "He that is unjust, let him be unjust still: and he which is filthy, let him be filthy still: and he that is righteous, let him be righteous still: and he that is holy, let him be holy still."

Our challenge and admonition in these times of turbulence, spiritual confusion and apostasy is to heed the living Word. We must take special notice of the last sentence, "he that is holy, let him be holy still."

Chapter 5

Introduction

The name Ephraim appears seven times in chapter 5; it means "fruitful." He is the second son of Joseph and Asenath, the daughter of Potipherah, born during the seven years of plenty in Egypt. In the book of Hosea, the name Ephraim does not exclusively identify the tribe of Ephraim, but in particular, the ten-tribe Israel. Often, the names Ephraim and Israel are interchangeable. This chapter also mentions the name Judah five times. This is a prophetic shadow of Ephraim's demise on the one hand, and their identity kept in Judah on the other.

The Prophet's Predicament

When reading the book of Hosea and the other prophets, we quickly come to the conclusion that they had the most unpleasant task. Not surprisingly, many were mistreated, imprisoned, even killed, because the judgment they proclaimed was for the future and not manifested visibly at the moment.

Israel considered themselves to be specially blessed; after all, they were the chosen of God. They were familiar with Scriptures such as Deuteronomy 14:2: "For thou art an holy people unto the LORD thy God, and the LORD hath chosen thee to be a peculiar people unto himself, above all the nations that are upon the earth." Therefore, when the prophets came proclaiming severe judgment, Israel did not believe it—they had all the proof that they were blessed.

The Rich Church

Let's look at a New Testament example, the testimony of a very prosperous and blessed church: "I am rich, and increased with goods, and have need of nothing" (Revelation 3:17). I think this is what we can say about most of our churches today. We drive comfortably in our heated or air conditioned car to church. There we find a building well-equipped, heated and air conditioned, with great comfort. Those who are physically handicapped are ushered in professionally. Biblical instruction is offered in many classes for virtually all age groups. Even the very little ones are expertly taken care of in the church nursery.

Besides, we have a large missionary budget, and virtually every year the budget is met, often above and beyond. So, what's wrong? Nothing that is visibly manifested.

But now let's take a look at how the Lord sees that same successful church: "I know thy works, that thou art neither cold nor hot: I would thou wert cold or hot. So then because thou art lukewarm, and neither cold nor hot, I will spue thee out of my mouth...and knowest not that thou art wretched, and miserable, and poor, and blind, and naked" (Revelation 3:15-16,17b). This shows the two different views: the visible, physical reality of our lives in the flesh, and the spiritual reality as viewed from heavenly perspectives.

"God Bless Israel"

If any one nation had the right to justifiably say that they are blessed, then doubtless it was the nation of Israel. Now comes the prophet Hosea, whose name means "Deliverer." Who needs a deliverer when things are going well? That is the sore point; it revealed Israel's failure to realize their spiritual condition.

Before we study these 15 verses in more detail, it is important to re-emphasize that God's message is one: it is a compact message from Genesis to Revelation. Such is also the case in the book of Hosea. Although severe judgments are proclaimed, yet we read at the end, "I will heal their backsliding, I will love them freely: for mine anger is turned away from him" (Hosea 14:4). Judgment and grace are intertwined.

Judgment against Priest and King

Terrible judgments come upon those who refused to heed God's commandment and instruction:

Hosea 5:1-2: "Hear ye this, O priests; and hearken, ye house of Israel; and give ye ear, O house of the king; for judgment is toward you, because ye have been a snare on Mizpah, and a net spread upon Tabor. 2 And the revolters are profound to make slaughter, though I have been a rebuker of them all."

Judgment is pronounced unabatedly, particularly against the priests and the king. Mizpah was the place where Jacob set up a stone pillar as a witness between his uncle Laban and himself, "And Mizpah; for he [Laban] said,

The LORD watch between me and thee, when we are absent one from another" (Genesis 31:49). Thus, Mizpah is a deciding point, a place of separation; but here, Mizpah is mentioned as a "snare." That means misuse; obviously, to their own advantage.

Tabor is the place in Israel where Deborah sent Barak to defeat the enemy Sisera. Here in this verse, Mizpah and Tabor are mentioned for the last time in the Bible. These places of decision and victory were misused religiously and politically by Israel.

Why Ephraim Is Israel

Hosea 5:3: "I know Ephraim, and Israel is not hid from me: for now, O Ephraim, thou committest whoredom, and Israel is defiled."

(See) Psalm 90:8; Amos 3:2

The often-repeated name Ephraim is considered to be special among the tribes of Israel. It was Ephraim who received the right hand of blessing from his grandfather Jacob: "And Israel stretched out his right hand, and laid it upon Ephraim's head, who was the younger, and his left hand upon Manasseh's head, guiding his hands wittingly; for Manasseh was the firstborn" (Genesis 48:14).

Ephraim, the most beloved, is representative of the people of Israel.

The Great Fall

Hosea 5:4-5: "They will not frame their doings to turn unto their God: for the spirit of whoredoms is in the midst of them, and they have not known the LORD. 5 And the pride of Israel doth testify to his face: therefore shall Israel and Ephraim fall in their iniquity; Judah also shall fall with them."

Again, devastation and horrible judgment from God is pronounced against Israel; but, we note, against Judah as well. Judah permitted the spirit of whoredom and pride in their midst. In other words, Judah was not guiltless; they took part in practicing idolatry.

Hosea 5:6: "They shall go with their flocks and with their herds to seek the LORD; but they shall not find him; he hath withdrawn himself from them."

They are seeking the Lord, but they will not find Him. This sounds contradictory, for the Lord patiently and compassionately invites people to come to Him. But here, He withdraws Himself; He will not be found. Why?

Hosea 5:7: "They have dealt treacherously against the LORD: for they have begotten strange children: now shall a month devour them with their portions."

(See) Ezekiel 12:28; Zechariah 11:8

Who Are the "Strange Children"?

Doubtless, this is a picture of their extreme whoredom: idolatry. A "strange child" is one who does not know his father. Israel brought forth "strange children," who did not know their Father which is in heaven. They alienated themselves from God, and God withdraws Himself from them.

> **Hosea 5:8-10:** "Blow ye the cornet in Gibeah, and the trumpet in Ramah: cry aloud at Bethaven, after thee, O Benjamin. 9 Ephraim shall be desolate in the day of rebuke: among the tribes of Israel have I made known that which shall surely be. 10 The princes of Judah were like them that remove the bound: therefore I will pour out my wrath upon them like water."

(See) Deuteronomy 19:14; Joshua 7:2

Besides Ephraim, we also read of Judah again, confirming Judah's falling away from God: they "remove the bound." That means the border between the rebellious ten-tribe Israel and the tribe of Judah could no longer be recognized.

Commandments of Man

Yet, we sense that in the midst of the proclamation of judgment, God is still seeking someone who has not kept company with the works of abomination practiced in Israel and Judah. However, their desire to follow man's ways is evident:

Hosea 5:11: "Ephraim is oppressed and broken in judgment, because he willingly walked after the commandment."

(See) 1 Kings 12:28

Speaking of the commandment, Luther uses the words, "commandments of man." Through the prophet Isaiah, the Lord reveals additional information: "Wherefore the Lord said, Forasmuch as this people draw near me with their mouth, and with their lips do honour me, but have removed their heart far from me, and their fear toward me is taught by the precept of men" (Isaiah 29:13).

Instead of Salvation, Condemnation

This tendency to follow God, mixed with the commandments of man, is just as popular today as it was in Hosea's time. But, the result of manmade laws and commandments is described in verses 12-14:

Hosea 5:12-14: "Therefore will I be unto Ephraim as a moth, and to the house of Judah as rottenness. 13 When Ephraim saw his sickness, and Judah saw his wound, then went Ephraim to the Assyrian, and sent to king Jareb: yet could he not heal you, nor cure you of your wound. 14 For I will be unto Ephraim as a lion, and as a young lion to the house of Judah: I, even I, will tear and go away; I will take away, and none shall rescue him."

God does not spare; there is no good news for evil deeds.

57

There is no hope of mercy for those who deliberately oppose God. Instead of help comes destruction; instead of salvation comes damnation.

Judah the Lion

We note that the house of Judah is mentioned again. Here we are reminded of the wonderful prophecy Jacob made about Judah: "Judah is a lion's whelp: from the prey, my son, thou art gone up: he stooped down, he couched as a lion, and as an old lion; who shall rouse him up?" (Genesis 49:9). The lion symbolizes royal power. In Revelation 5:5 we read, "the Lion of the tribe of Judah, the Root of David, hath prevailed." But here, the lion becomes a form of judgment against Judah and Israel.

The Wrath of the Lamb

This is the other side of the story. Such we read in Revelation 6, where the people of the earth, rich and poor, free and bond, "hid themselves in the dens and in the rocks of the mountains; And said to the mountains and rocks, Fall on us, and hide us from the face of him that sitteth on the throne, and from the wrath of the Lamb" (verses 15-16). The "Lamb of God, which taketh away the sin of the world," has now become the object of terrible fear.

Finally, we read in verse 15:

Hosea 5:15: "I will go and return to my place, till they acknowledge their offence, and seek my face: in their affliction they will seek me early."

God withdraws from His people. But there is one small spark of hope in the last sentence: "in their affliction they will seek me early."

May God grant that each of us will seek the Lord now; whether in affliction or out of affliction, whether in poverty or abundance. We are called to come closer to Him *now.* Hebrews 3:15 warns: "Today, if ye will hear his voice, harden not your hearts."

Chapter 6

Introduction

Chapter 6 opens with a ray of hope, "let us return unto the LORD." There is a remnant seeking the Lord. That's why in the end, the proclamation of judgment from the Lord will reveal mercy.

Recognition of God's patience, mercy and grace is evident in this first verse. Israel realizes that punishment comes from God, but healing will also come from Him.

"He Hath Torn"

Hosea 6:1: "Come, and let us return unto the LORD: for he hath torn, and he will heal us; he hath smitten, and he will bind us up."

(See) Exodus 15:26; Job 5:18; Isaiah 30:26; Jeremiah 30:17; Ezekiel 34:16

This is clearly in reference to the previous chapter, in verses 14-15, where God declares that He is the One who does the tearing, then He will go away. Yet the conclusion was, "they will seek me early." Some people in Israel clearly recognized that the predicament they found themselves in was due to their own violation of God's laws.

"The Third Day"

Next comes a significant prophetic statement:

Hosea 6:2: "After two days will he revive us: in the third day he will raise us up, and we shall live in his sight."

We know that one day with the Lord can be as a thousand years, and a thousand years as one day. More than 2,000 years ago, Jesus departed from Jerusalem and ascended into heaven from the Mount of Olives.

Luther actually translates this, "He will resurrect us to life after two days." Apply this to Israel; for the first time in about two thousand years, Israel is being raised up. They came to life as a political identity against all odds. They are a nation again. This actually did happen on 14 May 1948. Although still in unbelief until this very day, Israel is arising as a nation in spite of seemingly insurmountable difficulties: "in the third day he will raise us up." We can be assured that God is not finished with Israel.

Israel's Resurrection

The prophet Ezekiel speaks of the vision of dry bones. Reading chapter 37, we notice that the prophecy is directed to the dead, "dry bones." For 2,000 years, Israel had absolutely no chance and no hope of becoming a functioning nation. "Then he said unto me, Son of man, these bones are the whole house of Israel: behold, they say, Our bones are dried, and our hope is lost: we are cut off for our parts" (Ezekiel 37:11). There was no hope; it was impossible for Israel to be reborn as a nation. Yet we all know it did happen.

Here we learn God's plan for Israel: the first step is the return of the people to their land. The next step is the return of God to His people. Ezekiel 37:14 reads: "And shall put my spirit in you, and ye shall live."

Resurrection of the Land

We need to keep this succession in mind: the Jews came back in unbelief to the land of Israel. As a matter of fact, the establishment of the nation of Israel was primarily due to security, not religion. The largest group of people came from the communist Soviet Union. The first thing they did was to establish a collective farm settlement, based on the Soviet kolkhoz system, in Hebrew kibbutz.

The religious nations, particularly the USA, took no interest in establishing the Jewish State in Israel. As a matter of fact, they had an arms embargo against the Middle East. Thus, we read in *Outpost*, May 2005, page 9:

> The major Arab armies invading Palestine in 1948 were either British-led, trained and supplied (Egypt, Iraq and Trans-Jordan) or French equipped (Syria). Israel's victory owed much to heavy equipment mostly provided by the Soviet Union and Czechoslovakia (including the rifles the Czech army would have used to defend the homeland had Czechoslovakia not been betrayed by the Munich agreement). In contrast, the American State Department declared an embargo on all weapons and war material to both Jews and Arabs in Palestine—but not to the Arab states which sent in their forces to crush the Jewish state. The embargo substantively affected one side— those sympathetic to the Zionists who were forced to smuggle weapons to the beleaguered nascent Jewish army.

Interestingly, the Soviet Union supplied arms to the Jews. The rest of the world was just standing by, watching. They believed they were witnessing the founding and the death of the nation of Israel in May 1948. But the opposite happened.

Although we may not place too great a priority on this particular date or the event, we know for sure that what God has promised He will bring to pass. Israel in Hosea's time knew that something would happen "after two days."

Also, we see an analogy here of our Lord, who arose from the dead "on the third day." We read the testimony of the two disciples on their way to Emmaus, telling the risen Lord: "But we trusted that it had been he which should have redeemed Israel: and beside all this, to day is the third day since these things were done" (Luke 24:21). Jesus rose *on* the third day, not *after* the third day!

Israel's Glorious Hope

Hosea 6:3: "Then shall we know, if we follow on to know the LORD: his going forth is prepared as the morning; and he shall come unto us as the rain, as the latter and former rain unto the earth."

(See) Job 29:23; Proverbs 2:1, 9; Matthew 13:11

Occupying themselves with the prophetic Word caused them to realize that they are now on the right track. However, there is one problem: they used a futuristic expression, "Then shall we know," and, "shall come unto us." Apparently, they believed in the prophetic Word, but they placed it in the future; not now, but later.

God's Questions

Hosea 6:4-5: "O Ephraim, what shall I do unto thee? O Judah, what shall I do unto thee? For your goodness is as a morning cloud, and as the early dew it goeth away. 5 Therefore have I hewed them by the prophets; I have slain them by the words of my mouth: and thy judgments are as the light that goeth forth."

(See) Jeremiah 1:10; Hebrews 4:12

This apparent revival was short-lived, as is clearly expressed in verse 4: "For your goodness is as a morning cloud, and as the early dew it goeth away." Here Luther's translation says "for your love" instead of "goodness." This is confirmed also in verse 6, where God reveals that He is not looking for a sacrifice or burnt offering, but love (mercy).

Irreversible Judgment

Judgment was apparently irreversible. The prophets proclaimed it unsparingly. It is the power of the Lord Jesus Christ to make an end of Antichrist: "whom the Lord shall consume with the spirit of his mouth, and shall destroy with the brightness of his coming" (2 Thessalonians 2:8).

Here is what God desires:

Hosea 6:6: "For I desired mercy, and not sacrifice; and the knowledge of God more than burnt offerings."

(See) Psalm 50:8; Proverbs 21:3; Matthew 12:7; John 17:3

Knowing God's Way

Moses already proclaimed this in Deuteronomy 6:5: "And thou shalt love the LORD thy God with all thine heart, and with all thy soul, and with all thy might." To love the Lord is the key until this day.

Knowing God means to know His intention. David explains this in Psalm 103:7: "He made known his ways unto Moses, his acts unto the children of Israel." Israel saw the works of God, the mighty wonders, but did not understand. Moses, however, did understand; he had the knowledge of God.

Uncovering Sin

Once again, the prophet does not hesitate to enumerate the details of the horrible, sinful behavior of his people:

Hosea 6:7-10: "But they like men have transgressed the covenant: there have they dealt treacherously against me. 8 Gilead is a city of them that work iniquity, and is polluted with blood. 9 And as troops of robbers wait for a man, so the company of priests murder in the way by consent: for they commit lewdness. 10 I have seen an horrible thing in the house of Israel: there is the whoredom of Ephraim, Israel is defiled."

Note that the priests are targeted here; they have become

65

PROPHECY FOR TEN-TRIBE ISRAEL

"robbers" and "murderers" for gain.

Judah Included

Hosea 6:11: "Also, O Judah, he hath set an harvest for thee, when I returned the captivity of my people."

(See) Psalm 126:1

This refers to Judah's judgment; they will reap what they have sown. But at the same time, Israel's redemption is prophesied, "when I returned the captivity of my people."

The prophet Joel too speaks of that time: "For, behold, in those days, and in that time, when I shall bring again the captivity of Judah and Jerusalem" (Joel 3:1).

Israel, Our Example

Israel, as we all know, is given to us believers as an example. What happened to them physically, literally, and geographically is happening to us spiritually. Paul reveals this in Ephesians 6:12: "For we wrestle not against flesh and blood, but against principalities, against powers, against the rulers of the darkness of this world, against spiritual wickedness in high places." What must we do? Should we fight the powers of darkness? Not at all; we are to do one thing, and that is stand: "Wherefore take unto you the whole armour of God, that ye may be able to withstand in the evil day, and having done all, to stand" (verse 13).

That's the key: "standing." Having put on the whole

armor of God, we stand in faith, testifying that Jesus is the Victor; that is our calling. We do not have a chance fighting against the darkness, the spiritual wickedness and principalities. That is not our calling, because the battle has already been won by the Lord. Therefore, I emphasize one more time, stand and do the work as instructed in Ephesians 6:18: "Praying always with all prayer and supplication in the Spirit, and watching thereunto with all perseverance and supplication for all saints."

The "saints" represent the nation we should be most concerned about. That nation is called a "holy nation" in 1 Peter 2:9. "God bless this Church" is more appropriate than "God bless our nation."

Chapter 7

Introduction

This chapter reveals the most horrible sin, expressed with the words, "They have spoken lies against me...they rebel again me...they imagine mischief against me." It is no longer Israel's sin against God's commandments, but much worse: it's directly against God. This is repeatedly expressed with the words "against me." This outright rebellion against the living God causes judgment to be pronounced.

Limiting God

Hosea 7:1: "When I would have healed Israel, then the iniquity of Ephraim was discovered, and the wickedness of Samaria: for they commit falsehood; and the thief cometh in, and the troop of robbers spoileth without."

God's intention is clearly revealed by His words, "I would have healed Israel." But then the conflict is exposed: God's love makes Him yearn for His children Israel, yet God's righteousness requires punishment.

The Psalmist testifies to this controversy in Psalm 78:41: "Yea, they turned back and tempted God, and limited the Holy One of Israel." God could not fulfill His intention with Israel because they "limited the Holy One." Israel was destined to be above all the nations of the world, "For thou art an holy people unto the LORD

68

thy God, and the LORD hath chosen thee to be a peculiar people unto himself, above all the nations that are
upon the earth" (Deuteronomy 14:2). But now, judgment and destruction stand at the door.

Hosea 7:2: "And they consider not in their hearts that I remember all their wickedness: now their own doings have
beset them about; they are before my face."

(See) Psalm 90:8; Proverbs 5:22

The people of Israel had become so self-centered that
they simply did not believe in the fact that the God of Israel sees, hears and knows all things.

At the time of this proclamation against the people of
Israel, they were doing rather well. They were not suffering; freedom and prosperity prevailed. This is revealed
in the next verse:

Hosea 7:3: "They make the king glad with their wickedness,
and the princes with their lies."

(See) Romans 1:32

"As the people, so are the leaders." This saying is applicable here.

The Baker Analogy

Next, we read of the analogy of a baker. Most young
people know little about this. To bake bread in olden
time was quite an art; one had to be dedicated, giving

full attention to the process. Otherwise, the bread could not be used for food.

Hosea 7:4-7: "They are all adulterers, as an oven heated by the baker, who ceaseth from raising after he hath kneaded the dough, until it be leavened. 5 In the day of our king the princes have made him sick with bottles of wine; he stretched out his hand with scorners. 6 For they have made ready their heart like an oven, whiles they lie in wait: their baker sleepeth all the night; in the morning it burneth as a flaming fire. 7 They are all hot as an oven, and have devoured their judges; all their kings are fallen: there is none among them that calleth unto me."

(See) 2 Kings 15:10; Psalm 106:35; Isaiah 9:13

The saying, "Eat, drink and be merry" was the guideline for that day. Menge translates verse 5: "On the day of our king's birthday, the princes made themselves sick with the heat of the wine." This was party time, with subsequent immoral activity. There was blatant disregard for decency and authority, "devoured their judges; all their kings are fallen."

Worst of all is they totally ignore the God of Israel, "There is none among them that calleth unto me."

Heathen Behavior

Now Ephraim is highlighted again. This is not speaking about the tribe of Ephraim exclusively, but as we have seen previously, this speaks of the entire nation of Israel.

Hosea 7:8-9: "Ephraim, he hath mixed himself among the people; Ephraim is a cake not turned. 9 Strangers have devoured his strength, and he knoweth it not: yea, gray hairs are here and there upon him, yet he knoweth not."

We know that Israel was called to be separated unto the Lord, to be a holy people unto Him, yet here we read that Israel mixed with the heathen; subsequently, they lost the strength which was theirs, given by God based on His election.

In the end, as the result of their rebellion against God, they were no longer separated but scattered among the heathen, as Leviticus 26:33 testifies: "...I will scatter you among the heathen, and will draw out a sword after you: and your land shall be desolate, and your cities waste."

Again, we note Israel's obliviousness regarding their state: "Yet he knoweth not."

Hosea 7:10: "And the pride of Israel testifieth to his face: and they do not return to the LORD their God, nor seek him for all this."

Their own behavior was a testimony to their terrible predicament. Yet again, they do not seek the Lord.

Animal-like Behavior

Hosea 7:11-12: "Ephraim also is like a silly dove without heart: they call to Egypt, they go to Assyria. 12 When they shall go, I will spread my net upon them; I will bring them down as the fowls of the heaven; I will chastise them, as their congregation hath heard."

(See) Leviticus 26:14-39

We know that birds, or for that matter, all animals do not have a spirit; they cannot reason. Some time ago, I was reminded of that fact when my youngest son Simon went goose hunting. Well-camouflaged, firearms loaded, the four hunters suddenly saw a flock of geese flying overhead. After they emptied their guns into the flock, taking out quite a few, they knew that a few minutes later, the remnant geese would make another swoop down into the deathtrap, and then another one. They had not learned that they were flying right to their deaths.

Thus, the behavior of Israel is compared to a dove without a heart, without a spirit. They should know better than to go back to the deathtrap: Egypt and Assyria.

Wrong Escape

Next comes a threefold accusation against Israel:

Hosea 7:13: "Woe unto them! For they have fled from me: destruction unto them! Because they have transgressed against me: though I have redeemed them, yet they have spoken lies against me."

Fleeing from the Lord is a transgression, and so is speaking lies. In spite of the statement, "I have redeemed them," Israel continues practicing lies. That is blatant re-

72

bellion against God. This is not just a disregard for God's law, but a very deliberate challenge against the God of Israel. That is what the Gentile nations have done in the past, and will do in the future. Psalm 2 highlights the world's rebellion with the words, "against the Lord, and against his anointed."

Heartless Religion

Hosea 7:14: "And they have not cried unto me with their heart, when they howled upon their beds: they assemble themselves for corn and wine, and they rebel against me."

(See) Job 35:9; Psalm 78:34-37; Isaiah 29:13; Jeremiah 3:10

Apparently, they did pray to God, but here it is revealed that they did not do so in truth, "with their heart." Instead of seeking the Lord and repenting with their heart, they were totally occupied with their riches and well-being, "corn and wine." Thus the verdict, "They rebel against me."

In spite of God's innumerable miraculous interventions favoring Israel, they opposed Him:

Hosea 7:15: "Though I have bound and strengthened their arms, yet do they imagine mischief against me."

One more time, Israel tries superficially to repent, but in vain:

Hosea 7:16: "They return, but not to the most High: they are like a deceitful bow: their princes shall fall by the sword for the rage of their tongue: this shall be their derision in the land of Egypt."

(See) Psalm 73:9

As result of their actions, they became an object of ridicule in the land of Egypt, and later in the entire world.

When we read this chapter prayerfully, we recognize with great alarm that such behavior is prevalent in the church today. There is much activity, but little repentance of heart. Great and solemn resolutions are made, but in the end, they mostly turn out "against me [God]." Not without reason do we read in the New Testament the very serious warning, "Now these things were our examples, to the intent we should not lust after evil things, as they also lusted" (1 Corinthians 10:6).

Therefore, today, prove your heart; check your thoughts and see if the priority in your life is really the Lord Jesus Christ.

While Israel claimed to know God, their actions proved the opposite. The result was Israel's dispersion "among the Gentiles, as a vessel wherein is no pleasure" (Hosea 8:8). Religious Israel was led astray by their own imagination of heart, which led to them following other gods.

Chapter 8

Introduction

Relentlessly, the prophet exposes Israel's sins and declares destructive judgment. In particular, their hypocrisy is exposed. They were religiously very active, sacrificing, even confessing, "My God, we know thee." Yet the last verse thunders the truth, "Israel hath forgotten his Maker."

He Must Know Me

Hosea 8:1-2: "Set the trumpet to thy mouth. He shall come as an eagle against the house of the LORD, because they have transgressed my covenant, and trespassed against my law. 2 Israel shall cry unto me, My God, we know thee."

(See) Psalm 78:34; Jeremiah 4:13; Habakkuk 1:8; Matthew 7:21

When reading the words, "My God, we know thee," we are reminded of an unnamed group of people who come to the Lord confessing that they know Him, proudly enumerating the works they had done in His name. Yet there is a problem, because the Lord Himself said, "I never knew you: depart from me, ye that work iniquity" (Matthew 7:23).

Here we learn that to say we know the Lord is apparently not sufficient, because the Lord must also know us.

I can learn the Bible by heart, be educated in the finest seminaries in the world, write great books about Jesus, and present powerful sermons to multitudes, yet it will not help me one iota unless Jesus knows me.

How can I be sure that the Lord knows me? There's only one answer, and that is total, absolute and unconditional surrender to Him. Surrender also means being a "loser." Admitting that I am such a failure, a misfit, places me in the sphere of grace. That's the work of the Holy Spirit, who makes us recognize our hopeless position and condition.

When I come to Jesus, something remarkable happens: He accepts me, "Him that cometh to me, I will in no wise cast out." Coming to Jesus results in being born again of His Spirit, becoming a new person, a member of His body. From that point onward, I become an eternal identity. The Lord knows me very intimately, and I learn to know Him more and more.

The Apostle Paul knew of this relationship when he confessed in Philippians 3:10: "That I may know him, and the power of his resurrection, and the fellowship of his sufferings, being made conformable unto his death." We all know that Paul knew Christ very well. Paul is the author of most of the teaching books of the New Testament, but he makes it clear in this verse that he wants to know Him *more.*

The Truth of the Cross

Contrary to the general perception that when we become Christians, everything will run smoothly, that was definitely not the case with the Apostle Paul. He went from being a respected Bible scholar, a good and upright citizen, to one who was persecuted, rejected, beaten and put into prison. That's not very comforting. Paul even prays to be made "conformable unto His death."

Identifying Sin

When we read the words, "Set the trumpet to thy mouth," we have to understand that it does not speak of a physical trumpet, but the trumpet of the prophet's voice. Isaiah 58:1 reads: "Cry aloud, spare not, lift up thy *voice like a trumpet*, and show my people their transgression, and the house of Jacob their sins."

Prosperity Deception

Reading the next two verses, we understand again that Israel was experiencing prosperity:

Hosea 8:3-4: "Israel hath cast off the thing that is good: the enemy shall pursue him. 4 They have set up kings, but not by me: they have made princes, and I knew it not: of their silver and their gold have they made them idols, that they may be cut off."

(See) 1 Kings 12:16-20; 2 Kings 15:13, 17, 25

They rejected God and chose their own kings, who did not serve the Lord. They made themselves leaders without consulting the Lord. Worse yet, their riches, silver and gold became the means through which Israel worshiped idols; they became fully indulged in idolatry.

77

Hosea 8:5: "Thy calf, O Samaria, hath cast thee off; mine anger is kindled against them: how long will it be ere they attain to innocency?"

(See) Jeremiah 13:27

Here we see the main thrust of the prophet's message is directed against Samaria, representing the rebellious, ten-tribe kingdom of Israel. The last sentence Luther translates: "It cannot tarry long before they have to be punished."

Strangers Are Coming

During those days, Israel-Judah still had the temple intact, and a number of the kings of Judah served the Lord. Yet none of the kings of Israel urged their people to go to Jerusalem for worship.

Hosea 8:6-7: "For from Israel was it also: the workman made it; therefore it is not God: but the calf of Samaria shall be broken in pieces. 7 For they have sown the wind, and they shall reap the whirlwind: it hath no stalk: the bud shall yield no meal: if so be it yield, the strangers shall swallow it up."

We already mentioned that Israel was doing well, living in prosperity. However, that would change: they would sow much, but harvest little, and if there was some yield, foreigners would take it away.

Verse 8 makes an even stronger prophecy:

Hosea 8:8: "Israel is swallowed up: now shall they be among the Gentiles as a vessel wherein is no pleasure."

At the point of proclamation, Israel was not swallowed up; they were doing rather well, as indicated in verses 3-4. But from prophetic perspectives, it was already done. Israel was already "among the Gentiles" spiritually. History records that Israel was not accepted among the Gentiles, and indeed they became "a vessel wherein is no pleasure."

Destination: Assyria

The next three verses again reaffirm that the center of the message is directed toward the rebellious ten-tribe Israel:

Hosea 8:9-11: "For they are gone up to Assyria, a wild ass alone by himself: Ephraim hath hired lovers. 10 Yea, though they have hired among the nations, now will I gather them, and they shall sorrow a little for the burden of the king of princes. 11 Because Ephraim hath made many altars to sin, altars shall be unto him to sin."

(See) 2 Kings 15:19; Isaiah 10:8; Jeremiah 2:24; Ezekiel 16:33-34, 37

Israel-Ephraim acted exactly opposite of what the Lord had commanded them: they were to be separate, to segregate themselves from other nations. Yet here they attempt to merge with the nations; in this case, Assyria.

Friendship with the World

The *Tenakh* makes it a little clearer: "Ephraim has courted friendship. And while they are courting among the nations...." Friendship with the world means being an enemy of God. Isn't that what James 4:4 says? "Ye adulterers and adulteresses, know ye not that the friendship of the world is enmity with God? Whosoever therefore will be a friend of the world is the enemy of God."

Judah Diminished

The last part of verse 10 is in particularly revealing. While the King James translation says, "they shall sorrow a little for the burden of the king of princes," the *Tenakh* reads: "...they shall begin to diminish in number from the burden of king and officers." This is significant, because when we speak about the ten-tribe Israel, we know that they ceased to exist as a separate identity from Judah. They *diminished* when they were dispersed among the nations of the world.

Judah too was diminished. Historians tell us that over 14 million Jews were killed by the Gentiles, since the destruction of the Temple in Jerusalem in 70 A.D. The most horrendous act was committed by Hitler's Nazi regime, when they systematically murdered over 6 million Jews.

All this is part of God's declared destructive judgment upon Israel and Judah.

Hosea 8:12: "I have written to him the great things of my law, but they were counted as a strange thing."

(See) Deuteronomy 4:6; Nehemiah 9:13-14; Job 21:14; Proverbs 22:20;
Romans 3:1-2

The very words which God gave specifically to His people, became "a strange thing." They could no longer understand; they acted like animals, people without a spirit. This reminds us of Antichrist, who in Revelation is called the BEAST, or animal as other translations say.

Self-Serving Sacrifice

Hosea 8:13: "They sacrifice flesh for the sacrifices of mine offerings, and eat it; but the LORD accepteth them not; now will he remember their iniquity, and visit their sins: they shall return to Egypt."

This sacrifice was nothing other than self-pleasing, religious activity. God gives them up: "they shall return to Egypt." Often they expressed their desire, even in the beginning when they had escaped the slavery of Egypt, to return to Egypt. This tendency stayed with them until they were cast out from the Promised Land. For example, "We remember the fish, which we did eat in Egypt freely; the cucumbers, and the melons, and the leeks, and the onions, and the garlic" (Numbers 11:5).

Our Origin

We do well as believers to remember where we came from. Ephesians 2:11-12 reads: "Wherefore remember, that ye being in time past Gentiles in the flesh, who are called Uncircumcision by that which is called the Circumcision in the flesh made by hands; That at that time ye were without Christ, being aliens from the commonwealth of Israel, and strangers from the covenants of promise, having no hope, and without God in the world."

We were "aliens...having no hope, and without God in the world." This puts the lighthearted statements, "God's Country...God Bless America...In God We Trust," in clear opposition to God's Holy Word. It does not matter what nationality we belong to: without Christ, we have no hope. No slogan, no motto, no flag, no anthem will be of any help. These things we may be so proud of will become an object of shame when we shall see Him as He is.

Chapter 8 concludes with verse 14:

Hosea 8:14: "For Israel hath forgotten his Maker, and buildeth temples; and Judah hath multiplied fenced cities: but I will send a fire upon his cities, and it shall devour the palaces thereof."

(See) 1 Kings 12:31

At the time of this proclamation, Israel was building "temples," religious institutions, mighty buildings. Even Judah's economy was doing quite well; they constructed "fenced cities." The "Israeli dream" was fulfilled. They were religiously active and self-satisifying, but all without the God of Israel. They had "forgotten [their] Maker." Therefore, no matter how successful, how "blessed" we claim to be, it will all be exposed in the end as a great deception.

We repeat, there is no future for planet Earth, nor is

there hope for Israel outside the Lord God. Were it not for His mercy, grace, and compassion, we would be wasting our time even reading the prophets.

In conclusion of this chapter, let us highlight again God's immeasurable grace: "I will heal their backsliding, I will love them freely: for mine anger is turned away from him" (Hosea 14:4).

Chapter 9

Introduction

This chapter is a dark one; there is no light, no hope, no future. The statement of God, "I will love them no more," seals Ephraim-Israel's destiny. While there is a remnant of the ten-tribe rebellious Israel, as evident from other prophets and particularly from Revelation chapter 7, we have to reemphasize here that an independent ten-tribe Israel ceased to exist.

Ephraim

To begin, let us review the name Ephraim. This name plays a significant role, particularly in the book of Hosea, where it is mentioned 37 times.

Joseph had two sons in Egypt—Manasseh and Ephraim. Genesis 48:5 reads, "...thy two sons, Ephraim and Manasseh, which were born unto thee in the land of Egypt before I came unto thee into Egypt, are mine; as Reuben and Simeon, they shall be mine." Interestingly, the younger is mentioned first. When Jacob blessed these two sons, he deliberately puts his right hand on the head of the younger one—Ephraim. Thus, he gave him the greater blessing, as evident in verses 19-20: "...but truly his younger brother shall be greater than he, and his seed shall become a multitude of nations. And he blessed them that day, saying, In thee shall Israel bless, saying, God make thee as Ephraim and as Manasseh: and he set Ephraim before Manasseh."

Later in history, Moses too blesses Ephraim above Manasseh: "His glory is like the firstling of his bullock, and his horns are like the horns of unicorns: with them he shall push the people together to the ends of the earth: and they are the ten thousands of Ephraim, and they are the thousands of Manasseh" (Deuteronomy 33:17).

Scripture shows that Ephraim was definitely the favorite, the blessed one; thus, he became the very model of the ten-tribe nation of Israel.

However, when we read the last book of the Bible, Revelation, we notice that in chapter 7 Ephraim is missing, but Manasseh is mentioned.

The No-Hope Message

Hosea 9:1-2: "Rejoice not, O Israel, for joy, as other people: for thou hast gone a whoring from thy God, thou hast loved a reward upon every cornfloor. 2 The floor and the winepress shall not feed them, and the new wine shall fail in her."

Instead of riches, blessing and prosperity, poverty, famine and thirst is prophesied. Moreover, Ephraim-Israel shall be separated from the land of Israel:

Hosea 9:3-5: "They shall not dwell in the Lord's land; but Ephraim shall return to Egypt, and they shall eat unclean things in Assyria. 4 They shall not offer wine offerings to the LORD, neither shall they be pleasing unto him: their sacrifices shall be unto them as the bread of mourners; all that eat thereof shall be polluted: for their bread for their soul shall not come into the house of the LORD. 5 What will ye do in the solemn day, and in the day of the feast of the LORD?"

(See) Leviticus 18:25; Deuteronomy 4:26-27; 26:14; Ezekiel 4:13

This indicates their total separation from the promise of the inheritance of Israel. The "solemn day" and the "feast" are the signs of belonging to Israel; they are to be kept perpetually. But for Ephraim-Israel, who partook in the "unclean things of Assyria," it was the message of removal from the family of Israel.

Return to Egypt

This is particularly highlighted in the sentence, "Ephraim shall return to Egypt." Not surprisingly, Ephraim was born in Egypt. Now those who rebelled against Judah-Israel must return to where they came from.

Hosea 9:6-7: "For, lo, they are gone because of destruction: Egypt shall gather them up, Memphis shall bury them: the pleasant places for their silver, nettles shall possess them: thorns shall be in their tabernacles. 7 The days of visitation are come, the days of recompence are come; Israel shall know it: the prophet is a fool, the spiritual man is mad, for the multitude of thine iniquity, and the great hatred."

(See) Isaiah 19:13; 34:8; Jeremiah 2:16; Lamentations 2:14; Micah 7:4

Menge translates the first sentence of verse 6: "Behold!

They must wander to Assyria and Egypt; it will become their home and in Memphis shall they build their graves."

The Ten Lost Tribes

When we look for the ten lost tribes of Israel, we can find them in Egypt, in the countries of former Assyria, and in the rest of the world. Apparently, there is no return because "the prophet is a fool, the spiritual man is mad." The expression "fool" is a strong word and denotes a wicked and evil character, equivalent to a son of Bilial.

Madness indicates insanity, someone who does not have all his faculties functioning properly. More so, this is directed toward "the spiritual man," indicating loss of true spiritual connection with God.

Watchman and False Prophet

Hosea 9:8-9: "The watchman of Ephraim was with my God: but the prophet is a snare of a fowler in all his ways, and hatred in the house of his God. 9 They have deeply corrupted themselves, as in the days of Gibeah: therefore he will remember their iniquity, he will visit their sins."

We must take notice of the words "was with my God." This is written in the past tense; it's history. They once did belong. Note also the difference between "my God" and "his God." This indicates that the God of Israel was replaced with an idol. This is not a lighthearted thing.

Hosea 9:10: "I found Israel like grapes in the wilderness; I saw your fathers as the firstripe in the fig tree at her first time: but they went to Baalpeor, and separated themselves unto that shame; and their abominations were according as they loved."

(See) Deuteronomy 32:10; Numbers 25:3

God's love for ancient Israel is clearly expressed with the words, "grapes in the wilderness...firstripe in the fig tree." We know that God called Israel out of Egypt into the wilderness, where He spoke with them. Israel was to believe God, keep His commandments, and do all that He had instructed them. But we read the tragic words: "they went to Baalpeor." They went after idols, instead of separating themselves from the pagan nations and consecrating themselves to God. They "separated themselves unto that shame."

The End of Ephraim's Glory

We take note that all the 12 tribes of Israel are included, yet the target of the prophet who speaks the Word of God is Ephraim-Israel:

Hosea 9:11-12: "As for Ephraim, their glory shall fly away like a bird, from the birth, and from the womb, and from the conception. 12 Though they bring up their children, yet will I bereave them, that there shall not be a man left: yea, woe also to them when I depart from them!"

(See) Deuteronomy 31:17; 1 Samuel 28:15

Ephraim is being eradicated: no conception, no birth, "there shall not be a man left."

"I Will Love Them No More"

As if this is not enough, the prophet continues to thunder the message of judgment:

Hosea 9:13-16: "Ephraim, as I saw Tyrus, is planted in a pleasant place: but Ephraim shall bring forth his children to the murderer. 14 Give them, O LORD: what wilt thou give? Give them a miscarrying womb and dry breasts. 15 All their wickedness is in Gilgal: for there I hated them: for the wickedness of their doings I will drive them out of mine house, I will love them no more: all their princes are revolters. 16 Ephraim is smitten, their root is dried up, they shall bear no fruit: yea, though they bring forth, yet will I slay even the beloved fruit of their womb."

(See) Luke 23:29

These words are crystal clear: "I hated them...drive them out of mine house...love them no more...shall bear no fruit." That spells the utter end.

Here Tyrus is the model Ephraim-Israel follows in their rebellion against the God of Israel.

The End of Ten-Tribe Israel

We re-emphasize that while God targets these pronouncements of judgment against Ephraim, he includes all of Israel; in particular, the ten-tribe Israel, which rebelled against the tribe of Judah. Hence, they ceased to exist as a separate identity.

The last verse of chapter 9 reads:

Hosea 9:17: "My God will cast them away, because they did not hearken unto him: and they shall be wanderers among the nations."

(See) 2 Kings 17:18

This has been fulfilled for Ephraim-Israel, because they ceased to exist. Ephraim-Israel lost their inheritance and became Gentiles. Nevertheless, the remnant of the ten-tribe Ephraim-Israel returned to Judah and became Jews.

Chapter 10

Introduction

What a way to begin this chapter, "Israel is an empty vine." About halfway through we read, "...they shall say to the mountains, Cover us; and to the hills, Fall on us." God's declaration is clear: Ephraim-Israel is to be annihilated as an independent nation.

Reading the 15 verses of this chapter, we may search carefully for any sign of comfort or hope, but we will find little of it. The prophet continues his merciless message, exposing punishment for the sins of the people of Israel.

The Empty Vine

Hosea 10:1: "Israel is an empty vine, he bringeth forth fruit unto himself: according to the multitude of his fruit he hath increased the altars; according to the goodness of his land they have made goodly images."

(See) Isaiah 5:1-7; Ezekiel 15:1-6

Why is Israel an empty vine? Because it is self-centered, self-serving, and self-occupied. This empty vine nevertheless brings forth fruit, but different fruit; it is used to further idolatry. In other words, God's blessing, which the Israelites enjoyed, contributed toward their building more altars and manufacturing more idol images.

91

A Divided Heart

Hosea 10:2: "Their heart is divided; now shall they be found faulty: he shall break down their altars, he shall spoil their images."

(See) 1 Kings 18:21; Micah 5:13

It is evident from these words that Israel did not reject God altogether, but they worshiped idols at the same time. They had a divided heart. Subsequently, the Lord God had to cause the destruction of their altars and images, the very objects of their prosperity and blessings!

Hosea 10:3: "For now they shall say, We have no king, because we feared not the LORD; what then should a king do to us?"

(See) Psalm 12:4; Isaiah 5:19

It is evident from these words that the people recognized their sinfulness, "we feared not the LORD." Such being the case, what's the use of a king? Recognition of sin does not lead to repentance in this case.

The Ground Fails

Hosea 10:4: "They have spoken words, swearing falsely in making a covenant: thus judgment springeth up as hemlock in the furrows of the field."

(See) Deuteronomy 31:16-17; Ezekiel 17:13-19

Now the ground which produced prosperity becomes a snare: "Judgment springeth up as hemlock." The *Tenakh* reads: "Justice degenerates into poison weeds."

The Golden Calves
Next comes the center of their idolatry, namely the golden calves they had placed in Samaria and in Bethel:

Hosea 10:5-6: "The inhabitants of Samaria shall fear because of the calves of Bethaven: for the people thereof shall mourn over it, and the priests thereof that rejoiced on it, for the glory thereof, because it is departed from it. 6 It shall be also carried unto Assyria for a present to king Jareb: Ephraim shall receive shame, and Israel shall be ashamed of his own counsel."

(See) 1 King 12:28; 2 Kings 10:29

It seems significant that the writer does not say "Bethel," which means the "house of God," but "Bethaven," meaning "emptiness." These idols of Samaria and Bethaven will now be a present to their enemy, the king of Assyria. That surely is another highlight of Israel's shame. A nation so blessed with innumerable promises and a glorious future, becomes subject to idols and servant to an enemy nation.

End Time Judgment
The future of the royal kingdom and the two cities is de-

scribed with these words:

Hosea 10:7-8: "As for Samaria, her king is cut off as the foam upon the water. 8 The high places also of Aven, the sin of Israel, shall be destroyed: the thorn and the thistle shall come up on their altars; and they shall say to the mountains, Cover us; and to the hills, Fall on us."

(See) Deuteronomy 9:21; Revelation 6:16

This type of judgment is actually reserved for the end of the age, the Great Tribulation judgment. Thus, we read: "And the kings of the earth, and the great men, and the rich men, and the chief captains, and the mighty men, and every bondman, and every free man, hid themselves in the dens and in the rocks of the mountains" (Revelation 6:15).

Obviously, this caused Israel to have some feeling of guilt, due to the destruction of their object of worship and prosperity. But they would rather die than face the truth.

The book of Revelation identifies the reason why the people want to hide themselves behind the rocks and the mountains: "...hide us from the face of him that sitteth on the throne, and from the wrath of the Lamb" (Revelation 6:16). They are hiding "from the wrath of the Lamb." This is significant because the Lamb of God is the One who takes away the sins of the world, but not from the self-righteous who refuse to acknowledge their sin. During the Great Tribulation they will see Jesus, who could have saved them. They will be fully conscious of the fact that salvation is no longer available—it is eternally too late.

Double Sins

Hosea 10:9-10: "O Israel, thou hast sinned from the days of Gibeah: there they stood: the battle in Gibeah against the children of iniquity did not overtake them. 10 It is in my desire that I should chastise them; and the people shall be gathered against them, when they shall bind themselves in their two furrows."

(See) Deuteronomy 28:63; 1 Kings 14:16; Amos 8:14

Luther translates the last two words "two sins." What are the two sins or the "two furrows"? I think Jeremiah gives us a clue: "For my people have committed two evils; they have forsaken me the fountain of living waters, and hewed them out cisterns, broken cisterns, that can hold no water" (Jeremiah 2:13). Israel had forsaken the Lord God; that was bad enough. Worse, they created their own gods. Israel followed in the footsteps of the heathen nations. That was a slap in the face of the God of Israel, His teachings, and the words of the prophets.

Hosea 10:11: "And Ephraim is as an heifer that is taught, and loveth to tread out the corn; but I passed over upon her fair neck: I will make Ephraim to ride; Judah shall plow, and Jacob shall break his clods."

It is helpful to read the *Tanakh* here: "Ephraim became

a trained heifer, but preferred to thresh; I placed a yoke upon her sleek neck. I will make Ephraim do advance plowing; Judah shall do main plowing! Jacob shall do final plowing!" (verse 11). Ephraim, as we have repeatedly mentioned, represents the ten-tribe kingdom; Judah represents the Jews; and Jacob, the old flesh and blood nature. While this is primarily directed against the ten-tribe kingdom, we see once again that all of Israel is included.

All Life Is God-Given

The prophet is using examples from the farm to teach Israel a lesson. We all know that without agriculture, life on earth would cease to exist. The undomesticated animal world does not depend on agriculture, but they exist by the provision of the Creator. Animals exist without any planned agriculture. Man, in contrast, must work for food. Why? Because of the original sin. "...Cursed is the ground for thy sake; in sorrow shalt thou eat of it all the days of thy life; Thorns also and thistles shall it bring forth to thee; and thou shalt eat the herb of the field; In the sweat of thy face shalt thou eat bread, till thou return unto the ground; for out of it wast thou taken: for dust thou art, and unto dust shalt thou return" (Genesis 3:17-19).

God reminds Israel in no uncertain terms that in spite of all their work, their existence totally depends on Him.

This also shows how sin pollutes other people. Never take sin lightly, thinking it is hidden from others. That, quite apparently, is not the case; it does affect the entire Church. Here we see the effects of Israel's sin spreading to Judah.

A Spark of Hope

The next verse contains a small spark of hope nevertheless:

Hosea 10:12: "Sow to yourselves in righteousness, reap in mercy; break up your fallow ground: for it is time to seek the LORD, till he come and rain righteousness upon you."

(See) Isaiah 32:20; Proverbs 11:18; Ecclesiastes 11:6; James 3:18

In other words, if there is anyone yet in the land of Israel or Judah who is willing to serve the Lord with all his heart, with all his mind and strength, let him do it now. The time has come to "break up your fallow ground."

"Occupy Till I Come"

Do not permit the ground to be idle; you have work to do. The Lord has not placed you here on earth for you to simply enjoy life and be happy. There is a task to be accomplished; His will must yet be fulfilled: "Thy will be done in earth, as it is in heaven."

For Israel, this was just one more chance due to God's immeasurable grace, longsuffering and patience. One more time God says, "It is time to seek the Lord."

Vain Trust in Mighty Men

Hosea 10:13-14: "Ye have plowed wickedness, ye have

reaped iniquity; ye have eaten the fruit of lies: because thou didst trust in thy way, in the multitude of thy mighty men. 14 Therefore shall a tumult arise among thy people, and all thy fortresses shall be spoiled, as Shalman spoiled Betharbel in the day of battle: the mother was dashed in pieces upon her children."

(See) Job 4:8; Psalm 33:16; Proverbs 22:8; Isaiah 17:3; Galatians 6:7-8

During the time when the prophets proclaimed the truth of God's Word, Israel had plenty of food; they were secure because of the "multitude of...mighty men." Surely, they had nothing to worry about. After all, the prophets always proclaimed doomsday, so why listen to them? Soon, however, their error would find them out. Who is Shalman? The king of Assyria. Not even the mothers and little ones were spared, but they were dashed to pieces. What a horrible end they had come to!

Hosea 10:15: "So shall Bethel do unto you because of your great wickedness: in a morning shall the king of Israel utterly be cut off."

Once more, it is documented that the ten-tribe Israel has no future; their king shall "utterly be cut off." Israel no longer has a political identity as a kingdom separate from Judah, the royal tribe.

Chapter 11

Introduction

Another heart wrenching declaration of God's love for Ephraim. Four questions reveal God's conflict between His great love on the one hand, and His righteousness on the other. But a window of grace is open for a remnant. In contrast, Judah is established.

Israel My Son

Hosea 11:1: "When Israel was a child, then I loved him, and called my son out of Egypt."

(See) Exodus 4:22; Matthew 2:15

There is something revealing about this first verse of chapter 11; it is God's declaration and acknowledgement of His love for His people. It is addressed to all of Israel. This love is distinctly separate from the love God has for all His creation: "For God so loved the world."

Israel is different; as a nation they are incomparable to any other nation on the face of the earth. It is a grave error to take Israel's history and their relationship to God the Creator, and attempt to apply it to any other nation.

Herein lies the distinct difference, "Happy art thou, O Israel: who is like unto thee, people saved by the LORD, the shield of thy help, and who is the sword of thy excellency" (Deuteronomy 33:29). Note the two questions

Moses addresses to his people: "Did ever people hear the voice of God speaking out of the midst of the fire, as thou hast heard, and live? Or hath God assayed to go and take him a nation from the midst of another nation, by temptations, by signs, and by wonders, and by war, and by a mighty hand, and by a stretched out arm, and by great terrors, according to all that the LORD your God did for you in Egypt before your eyes?" (Deuteronomy 4:33-34).

God calls Israel "my son." This declaration was made in the land of Egypt: "And thou shalt say unto Pharaoh, Thus saith the LORD, Israel is my son, even my firstborn" (Exodus 4:22).

God's son is Israel and the Son of God is an Israelite, according to Matthew 2:15: "Out of Egypt have I called my son." The Lord Jesus Himself is identified with His people. Jesus was and is a Jew; He is an Israelite. He has not changed His nationality, nor will He ever. He is eternally, "The Lion of the tribe of Judah, the Root of David" (Revelation 5:5).

God's Offer of Restoration Rejected

Hosea 11:2-4: "As they called them, so they went from them: they sacrificed unto Baalim, and burned incense to graven images. 3 I taught Ephraim also to go, taking them by their arms; but they knew not that I healed them. 4 I drew them with cords of a man, with bands of love: and I was to them as they that take off the yoke on their jaws, and I laid meat unto them."

(See) Leviticus 26:13; 2 Kings 17:16; Isaiah 65:7; Jeremiah 18:15

Over and again, God reminds His people where they came from; bondage, slavery, suffering. Yet God's love is nevertheless manifested in the words, "I healed them. I drew them with cords of a man, with bands of love."

A Picture for the Church

That's one point where we may spiritualize these matters for the Church. Each of us who has come by faith to Jesus, asked forgiveness and, as a result, received the assurance of salvation through the rebirth, originates from such a hopeless position. Don't you ever believe that "there is a little good in everybody." That's the message of Lucifer. There is nothing good in you or me; there is nothing good in your family, your town or your country.

If we would only recognize the hopeless situation we are in without the Savior, the Lord Jesus Christ, we would be shocked beyond description.

Israel's Refusal of God's Love

The prophet describes in detail how Israel refused to heed His words. They sacrificed unto Balaam; they burned incense unto graven images. They did it deliberately and intentionally, violating His commandments.

One senses God's compassionate love for His people. He taught them to walk; He held them by their arms, but they did not acknowledge it. He drew them with cords of love and helped them carry the yoke of everyday life; He even gave them food to eat, but all in vain.

Israel's refusal to obey God and their stubborn insistence on doing their own will, caused them to become subject to the Assyrians. Their habitation was destroyed, including their security:

Hosea 11:5-6: "He shall not return into the land of Egypt, but the Assyrian shall be his king, because they refused to return. 6 And the sword shall abide on his cities, and shall consume his branches, and devour them, because of their own counsels."

(See) 2 Kings 17:13; Jeremiah 8:4-6; Amos 4:6; Zechariah 1:4

Stubborn Insistence to Backslide

Hosea: 11:7: "And my people are bent to backsliding from me: though they called them to the most High, none at all would exalt him."

They had made up their mind; they were tired of listening to the truth. Luther translates this verse, "My people have become tired to turn unto me: even if they are preached to, no one arises to take notice." When reading these verses, one senses the utter hopelessness in which Israel finds herself in relationship to God.

God's Compassion and Controversy

Hosea 11:8-9: "How shall I give thee up, Ephraim? How shall I deliver thee, Israel? How shall I make thee as Admah? How shall I set thee as Zeboim? Mine heart is turned within me, my repentings are kindled together. 9

I will not execute the fierceness of mine anger, I will not return to destroy Ephraim: for I am God, and not man; the Holy One in the midst of thee: and I will not enter into the city."

(See) Genesis 14:8; Deuteronomy 29:23; Malachi 3:6; Romans 11:29

Here we see God's great compassion; His love is clearly expressed, yet His righteousness must be implemented. His Law stands for ever; His judgments are irrevocable. Thus, He asks the questions: Is it possible for me to give up Ephraim? Is there a way to deliver Israel? Should I destroy them as Admah and Zeboim (places destroyed during the fire judgment upon Sodom and Gomorrah)? Indeed, God has a controversy, "mine heart is turned within me, my repentings are kindled together." We are reminded here of the words of Jeremiah 31:20: "Is Ephraim my dear son? Is he a pleasant child? For since I spake against him, I do earnestly remember him still: therefore my bowels are troubled for him; I will surely have mercy upon him, saith the LORD." Doubtless, this relates to the remnant of Israel.

Grace however, will break through nevertheless. This coming grace is a prophecy based on the fulfillment of judgment and justice; namely, the sacrifice of God's Son on Calvary's cross.

He "will not enter into the city" to destroy it as He did with Admah and Zeboim. In other words, the land of Israel will remain; it will not become as Sodom and Gomorrah.

The Ultimate Sacrifice

The sacrifices presented by the priest for the people were no longer effective, because they had continuously and persistently violated God's holy commandment.

Even in Judah, the sacrifices in the glorious temple on Mount Moriah in Jerusalem, the blood of innumerable animals, could in no way take away Israel's sin. It was only a temporary covering until the perfect Lamb of God came. John exclaims: "Behold the Lamb of God, which taketh away the sin of the world" (John 1:29). That was the only way to solve God's conflict; not only with Israel, but also with all of mankind. Hebrews 10:4 confirms: "For it is not possible that the blood of bulls and of goats should take away sins."

The Ultimate Law

If we begin to grasp this important fact with our spirit, we then realize what a horrendous insult it is when we think that by keeping certain Old Testament laws, we can please God. We, as believers of the New Covenant, have to answer to a much higher law; actually, infinitely higher than the Old Testament. Why? Because something more than the blood of goats and bulls was shed: the blood of the Son of God, the Sinless One, the perfect sacrifice. Here we should read Hebrews 9:12: "Neither by the blood of goats and calves, but by his own blood he entered in once into the holy place, having obtained eternal redemption for us."

Restoration Promised

Hosea 11:10-11: "They shall walk after the LORD: he shall roar like a lion: when he shall roar, then the children shall tremble from the west. 11 They shall tremble as a bird out of Egypt, and as a dove out of the land of Assyria: and I will place them in their houses, saith the LORD."

(See) Isaiah 31:4; 66:2, 5; Joel 3:16; Amos 1:2

God Himself will initiate the return of His children to their land. The *Tanakh* reads: "The LORD will roar like a lion, And they shall march behind Him; When He roars, His children shall come fluttering out of the west." We know that west of Israel is the Mediterranean. The overwhelming majority of Jews who have gone back home to the land of Israel, came either by boat or plane, from the west, over the Mediterranean, then landing in Israel.

Return in Unbelief

Now we come to a controversy within the camp of Bible scholars. One group says that the ingathering of the exiles will only take place when Israel repents; only then will God in His grace cause them to return to the land.

The other group believes that the Jews are to come back to the land of Israel in unbelief. The Jews' motivation to return is not to seek the Lord God, to establish the Old Covenant in the land of Israel; their motive is existence, identity, and security. Only a Jewish passport can give a Jew the needed security.

There are three reasons why the Jews are returning to the land of Israel in unbelief:

1. The Messiah, Jesus Christ, is going to come to Israel. To be precise, His feet shall stand on the Mount of Olives. When that occurs, the Jews will suddenly recognize Him. That means Jews have to be in the land of Israel in order to recognize the Messiah.

2. It would be impossible for the Jews to return to Israel unless the land is restored to productivity; otherwise, they would starve—no food, no life. Thus, the Jews did a remarkable job under the auspices of communism, establishing Kibbutzim (collective agriculture settlements) throughout the land. That assured food for the people. This corresponds to the prophecy we read in Ezekiel 36:8: "But ye, O mountains of Israel, ye shall shoot forth your branches, and yield your fruit to my people of Israel; for they are at hand to come."

3. The Jews who have returned in the past and who are still returning today, are establishing a political reality which condemns all the nations of the world for their injustice toward Jerusalem and the Promised Land. Jerusalem is the key by which the nations will be judged. While Israel insists that Jerusalem is the united capital city of the State of Israel, all nations, without exception, shout determinedly, "No!"

When Friends Are Foes

There is an abundance of documentation available showing the opposition of all nations to Israel taking possession of all of the city of Jerusalem. We know about the

Arabs and the Islamic nations, those who seek to destroy Israel. But we also need to look at those who claim to be friends of Israel, such as the EU and the US. Here the prophetic Word is crystal clear, "All nations before him are as nothing; and they are counted to him less than nothing, and vanity" (Isaiah 40:17). We may add the words of the prophet Joel, "I will also gather ALL nations..." (Joel 3:2).

Redemption through Judah

Hosea 11:12: "Ephraim compasseth me about with lies, and the house of Israel with deceit: but Judah yet ruleth with God, and is faithful with the saints."

The *Tanakh* reads: "Ephraim surrounds Me with deceit, The House of Israel with guile. But Judah stands firm with God and is faithful to the Holy One." Distinction is made between Ephraim-Israel and Judah-Israel, but salvation is based on God's grace alone.

Chapter 12

Introduction

Ephraim-Israel is faced with his past, reminded that the father of Israel is Jacob, the one who had "power with God...power over the angel, and prevailed." This is another challenge for the remnant of Israel to repent, to return, but the conclusion of this chapter reads, "...and his reproach shall his Lord return unto him."

Waiting for the Lord

Reading the 14 verses of Hosea 12, it is quite apparent that the word "wait" is center: "wait on thy God continually" (verse 6). That is what Israel was supposed to do. Had they waited for the Lord continually, they would have recognized the child born in Bethlehem.

This is also evident from the testimony of two people in Israel: first, the old man Simeon: "...The same man was just and devout, waiting for the consolation of Israel: and the Holy Ghost was upon him" (Luke 2:25). This man practiced "wait[ing] on [his] God continually."

Another person mentioned is Anna, a prophetess of the tribe of Asher. "And there was one Anna, a prophetess, the daughter of Phanuel, of the tribe of Aser: she was of a great age, and had lived with an husband seven years from her virginity; And she was a widow of about fourscore and four years, which departed not from the temple, but served God with fastings and prayers night and day. And she coming in that instant gave thanks likewise unto the Lord, and spake of him to all them that looked for redemption in Jerusalem" (Luke 2:36-38).

Why did they wait? The answer is simple: the prophets proclaimed the Messiah would come, and they believed the prophets.

If only we would do likewise. Our priority would be shifted from the things of this world to spiritual sustenance, such as can only be grasped by faith: "Now faith is the substance of things hoped for, the evidence of things not seen" (Hebrews 11:1).

Believing God's prophets is essential, "And by a prophet the LORD brought Israel out of Egypt, and by a prophet was he preserved" (Hosea 12:13). Waiting for the fulfillment of prophecy is key.

Ephraim-Israel Failed to Wait upon the Lord

Hosea 12:1: "Ephraim feedeth on wind, and followeth after the east wind: he daily increaseth lies and desolation; and they do make a covenant with the Assyrians, and oil is carried into Egypt."

(See) Genesis 41:6; Jeremiah 22:22; Ezekiel 17:10

When we consider that they followed the east wind, we realize that when you go east, you just go in circles. Where is east? That depends on where you are located. What the prophet is saying here is that Ephraim is running in circles. In this case, they trusted the Assyrians, who in the end destroyed them and exported Israel's precious cargo of oil or balsam to the land of Egypt.

PROPHECY FOR TEN-TRIBE ISRAEL

Jacob the Wrestler

Hosea 12:2: "The LORD hath also a controversy with Judah, and will punish Jacob according to his ways; according to his doings will he recompense him."

In conjunction with Judah, Jacob is mentioned; that is, the old flesh and blood nature of Israel.

Hosea 12:3-4: "He took his brother by the heel in the womb, and by his strength he had power with God: 4 Yea, he had power over the angel, and prevailed: he wept, and made supplication unto him: he found him in Bethel, and there he spake with us;"

(See) Genesis 25:26; 28:12; 32:28

This is a factual account, showing the literal contact between Jacob and God. Although Jacob was defeated, "Jacob's thigh was out of joint, as he wrestled with him," the Scripture states that he prevailed. That seems like a contradiction. How did he prevail? By his total surrender to the power of God. Jacob knew he was 100% dependent on God's grace; thus, he cried out, "I will not let thee go, except thou bless me." That defines prevailing. Verse 5 determines Jacob's position:

Hosea 12:5: "Even the LORD God of hosts; the LORD is his memorial."

In other words, Jacob, the very successful businessman,

on his way to his homeland, coming back with great riches, yet became a broken man totally dependent upon God.

Now we should better understand the words:

Hosea 12:6: "Therefore turn thou to thy God: keep mercy and judgment, and wait on thy God continually."

(See) Micah 6:8

Ephraim the Businessman

Hosea 12:7-8: "He is a merchant, the balances of deceit are in his hand: he loveth to oppress. 8 And Ephraim said, Yet I am become rich, I have found me out substance: in all my labours they shall find none iniquity in me that were sin."

(See) Proverbs 11:1; Amos 8:5; Micah 6:11; Revelation 3:17

The distinction is made that while Jacob humbled himself, Ephraim-Israel did not. Although corrupt through and through, using oppression and deceit, Ephraim proudly exclaims, "There is no iniquity, there is no sin in me."

Here we are reminded of one church, which proudly exclaims in Revelation 3:17: "I am rich, and increased with goods, and have need of nothing."

111

The God of Israel

Hosea 12:9: "And I that am the LORD thy God from the land of Egypt will yet make thee to dwell in tabernacles, as in the days of the solemn feast."

(See) Leviticus 23:42

The Lord shows Ephraim-Israel that it is He who permits him to "dwell in tabernacles."

Hosea 12:10: "I have also spoken by the prophets, and I have multiplied visions, and used similitudes, by the ministry of the prophets."

(See) 2 Kings 17:13; Jeremiah 7:25; Ezekiel 17:2; 20:49

Again, the prophetic Word is highlighted. God spoke to His people continually, in various ways and manners. This is confirmed in Hebrews 1:1: "God, who at sundry times and in divers manners spake in time past unto the fathers by the prophets." But note verse 2: "Hath in these last days spoken unto us by his Son...." These two verses clearly invalidate any and all claims of being God's prophet in our days. God spoke in times past, but in the last days, He has spoken to us by His Son. We have the full counsel of God in our possession—it's the Bible, from Genesis to Revelation. There is no need for additional revelation. His message to man through His Son is final and complete, perfect.

112

The Gilead Conflict

Hosea 12:11: "Is there iniquity in Gilead? Surely they are vanity: they sacrifice bullocks in Gilgal; yea, their altars are as heaps in the furrows of the fields."

(See) Amos 4:4

Gilead is the land along the Jordan River from the Sea of Galilee to the Dead Sea. It reaches Gilgal, the place where the Israelis camped first after they crossed the Jordan in their quest to take possession of the Promised Land. But look what Israel did: they sacrificed and built altars in unauthorized places. They deliberately acted in opposition to God's clear instruction, such as Deuteronomy 16:2, "Thou shalt therefore sacrifice the passover unto the LORD thy God, of the flock and the herd, in the place which the LORD shall choose to place his name there."

Again the prophet goes back to Jacob:

Hosea 12:12-13: "And Jacob fled into the country of Syria, and Israel served for a wife, and for a wife he kept sheep. 13 And by a prophet the LORD brought Israel out of Egypt, and by a prophet was he preserved."

(See) Genesis 28:5; 29:20

Jacob had to flee to Syria to escape from his twin brother Esau. On his return, he was transformed into Israel. His name was changed from "supplanter" to "God's fighter."

It was the Word of God Jacob received which preserved him: "there he spake with us." Through the prophetic Word, God led Israel out of the land of Egypt; through His prophetic Word, He has kept the Jewish people until this very day; and through the prophetic Word, Israel is being restored.

Ephraim's Perpetual Rebellion

In spite of the overwhelming evidence of God's providence for His people Israel, Ephraim continued to rebel:

Hosea 12:14: "Ephraim provoked him to anger most bitterly: therefore shall he leave his blood upon him, and his reproach shall his Lord return unto him."

(See) Deuteronomy 28:37; Daniel 11:18

This statement, "therefore shall he leave his blood upon him," indicates there is no remission for Ephraim. He made a covenant with death, with the Assyrians who carried him into final captivity. Ephraim, the symbol of the ten-tribe Israel, ceased to exist as an independent identity from Judah.

Eternal Citizens

We have a clear picture here of the world at large. The Gospel is being proclaimed to people all over the world, but very few actually hear and receive it. Who are these "few"? They are the elect; they have become eternal citizens, and will be in the presence of the Lord God for all eternity. All others will be eradicated; their names will be taken out of the Book of Life, and the knowledge of them shall cease. That, incidentally, is what Christ's coming to earth was and is all about: salvation to mankind, giving each and every one the opportunity to believe in the only Savior, in the only escape from Lucifer-dominated Earth. Have you made your decision yet?

Chapter **13**

Introduction

When we read the prophet Hosea, we are confronted with God's truth in opposition to man's acceptance of Satan's lies. We have to reiterate here that Israel is God's chosen people. The God of heaven revealed Himself to Israel in many unmistakable ways. They had all the proof in the world that God was and is real, that His Word is true, and that He always brings His promises to pass. Yet reading Hosea, we notice that Israel did not take heed, but did according to their own imagination of their evil heart.

What is evident in our days is the fact that truth and lie, light and darkness, are being mixed more than ever. As a matter of fact, it sometimes becomes difficult to judge whether what I read and hear is truth or only partial truth. Such developments should not surprise us, because when the disciples asked Jesus about the future, He gave a very sobering warning, "Take heed that no man deceive you."

Heights of Self-Esteem

Hosea 13:1: "When Ephraim spake trembling, he exalted himself in Israel; but when he offended in Baal, he died."

(See) 2 Kings 17:16; Proverbs 18:12

The various translations differ regarding the first sentence, "When Ephraim spake trembling, he exalted himself in Israel." Whether this means that he trembled at the Word of God or that he spoke great things—subsequently, exalted himself in Israel—is not quite clear. The last part, "when he offended in Baal, he died" is plain because he separated himself from the living God, and died in his sin of worshiping Baal.

"Kiss the Calves"

Hosea 13:2: "And now they sin more and more, and have made them molten images of their silver, and idols according to their own understanding, all of it the work of the craftsmen: they say of them, Let the men that sacrifice kiss the calves."

Idolatry was the accepted norm of religious activity during those days. All the heathen nations manufactured their own idols; thus, Israel did likewise.

We find variations in translations of the words, "Let the men that sacrifice kiss the calves." Luther translates it, "He who kisses the calves must sacrifice man." But in both cases, the message is clear: Ephraim-Israel committed abomination to the utmost. They totally surrendered to idolatry in a most hedonistic way.

Hosea 13:3: "Therefore they shall be as the morning cloud, and as the early dew that passeth away, as the chaff that is driven with the whirlwind out of the floor, and as the smoke out of the chimney."

117

(See) Psalm 1:4; 68:2; Isaiah 17:13

This is fulfillment of the words, "the soul that sinneth, it shall die." Judgment comes when the fullness of sin has been reached.

God Recalls His Actions for Israel

Hosea 13:4-6: "Yet I am the LORD thy God from the land of Egypt, and thou shalt know no god but me: for there is no saviour beside me. 5 I did know thee in the wilderness, in the land of great drought. 6 According to their pasture, so were they filled; they were filled, and their heart was exalted; therefore have they forgotten me."

(See) Exodus 20:3; Deuteronomy 8:12, 14; Isaiah 43:11; 45:21-22

The Lord God goes back to the beginning. He looks at the whole history of Israel. He was the One who brought Israel out of slavery from Egypt with a mighty hand. He made known His law through Moses. Israel should not have another god; only He is the Savior. Israel had absolutely no reason to depart from God. We read of this fact continually, not only in the book of Hosea but also in all the prophets. Yet they chose to forget what God had done for them, and instead of exalting the Lord, they exalted themselves. That is the climax of self-esteem.

Hosea 13:7-8: "Therefore I will be unto them as a lion: as a leopard by the way will I observe them: 8 I will meet them as a bear that is bereaved of her whelps, and will

118

rend the caul of their heart, and there will I devour them like a lion: the wild beast shall tear them."

(See) 2 Samuel 17:8; Jeremiah 5:6; Lamentations 3:10

We note the three animals, the lion, the leopard and the bear. This reminds us of the first night vision of the prophet Daniel, which pictured the four Gentile power structures that would devour the children of Israel. The first three, the lion, the bear, and the leopard, represented Babylon, Persia and Greece. The fourth beast is the epitome of evil: "After this I saw in the night visions, and behold a fourth beast, dreadful and terrible, and strong exceedingly; and it had great iron teeth: it devoured and brake in pieces, and stamped the residue with the feet of it: and it was diverse from all the beasts that were before it; and it had ten horns" (Daniel 7:7). Truly, Israel has experienced these judgments throughout their history.

Verse 9 seems as if the Lord interrupts Himself:

Hosea 13:9: "O Israel, thou hast destroyed thyself; but in me is thine help."

(See) Deuteronomy 33:26; Jeremiah 2:17

One senses God's compassion for His people, how He desires to help, to restore. Here we must recall chapter 11, verse 8: "How shall I give thee up, Ephraim? how shall I deliver thee, Israel? how shall I make thee as Admah? how shall I set thee as Zeboim? mine heart is turned within me, my repentings are kindled together."

God's Repeated Offer

One more time, God reveals His intention through His prophet, but to no avail:

Hosea 13:10-12: "I will be thy king: where is any other that may save thee in all thy cities? and thy judges of whom thou saidst, Give me a king and princes? 11 I gave thee a king in mine anger, and took him away in my wrath. 12 The iniquity of Ephraim is bound up; his sin is hid."

(See) Deuteronomy 32:24; 1 Samuel 8:7; 10:17-24; 15:26; Job 14:17; Romans 2:5

God reveals that He wants to be their king. He would judge righteously and protect, but they requested a king according to their own heart. God gave them King Saul, but He also took him away.

There is nothing left worth salvaging. Ephraim-Israel is, in modern words, a lost cause.

Hosea 13:13: "The sorrows of a travailing woman shall come upon him: he is an unwise son; for he should not stay long in the place of the breaking forth of children."

(See) Deuteronomy 32:6; Isaiah 13:8; 37:3; 66:9; Micah 4:9-10

Although a child not yet born has no power to be born, here God is revealing to us there is so much stubbornness in Ephraim that he chooses not to be born, not to be renewed, not to experience the rebirth.

A Ray of Hope

Then, suddenly, a ray of hope breaks through the clouds of dark judgment threatening to suffocate Israel:

Hosea 13:14: "I will ransom them from the power of the grave; I will redeem them from death: O death, I will be thy plagues; O grave, I will be thy destruction: repentance shall be hid from mine eyes."

(See) Isaiah 25:8; 26:19; 1 Corinthians 15:55; 1 Thessalonians 4:14-17

God Himself will be the enemy of death. The prophet Isaiah made a similar statement, "He will swallow up death in victory" (Isaiah 25:8).

Eternal Redemption

We are also reminded of the words found in the New Testament in 1 Corinthians 15:54-55: "So when this corruptible shall have put on incorruption, and this mortal shall have put on immortality, then shall be brought to pass the saying that is written, Death is swallowed up in victory. O death, where is thy sting? O grave, where is thy victory?" That is the ultimate fulfillment for each and every believer who has put his/her faith in the accomplished work of Jesus Christ on Calvary's Cross. Christ's redemption is complete, perfect, and valid for all eternity. That is what God makes known to His people through His prophets. The ultimate intention is not destruction, but salvation in Him. Nevertheless, we must not be carried away by God's grace and allow room for the assumption that He will ignore sin and rebellion. The end result of sin and rebellion is death and destruction. There are no two ways about it. But the one who seeks the Lord, who yearns for Him and allows the Holy Spirit to reveal the truth about one's self, recognizes his/her sin and failure before God. Such a one can already shout with trembling voice but deep conviction in his heart, "O death, where is thy sting? O grave, where is thy victory?"

Another East Wind

Hosea 13:15: "Though he be fruitful among his brethren, an east wind shall come, the wind of the LORD shall come up from the wilderness, and his spring shall become dry, and his fountain shall be dried up: he shall spoil the treasure of all pleasant vessels."

(See) Genesis 41:6; Jeremiah 20:5; 51:36

The word "fruitful" is referring to the name Ephraim, which means "double fruit." Yet it will not be lasting; "the wind of the Lord" will dry it up.

Samaria Instead of Jerusalem

Hosea 13:16: "Samaria shall become desolate; for she hath rebelled against her God: they shall fall by the sword: their infants shall be dashed in pieces, and their women with child shall be ripped up."

(See) 2 Kings 8:12; 15:16

Samaria attempted to supplant Jerusalem. In other words, Samaria became an imitation of the real thing. That is the most horrendous sin against the God of Israel.

We know that Israel was judged when Assyria conquered the land; the cities were destroyed, many people were killed, and the remnant were carried into captivity.

The most brutal expression is exhibited with the words, "their infants shall be dashed in pieces." This is a significant statement because when you take the infants away from a nation, that nation is doomed. Even worse, "their women with child shall be ripped up"; this shows that there is no mercy. When the infants die and the unborn will not see the light of day, then there is nothing but utter hopelessness for any nation. It's the ultimate end.

We must take note that this is addressed to Samaria; it doesn't say Israel or the ten-tribe kingdom, but targets Samaria. Why? Because those who went to Samaria, who had supported the rebellion against God's order, became one with the idolatry of Samaria. The word "Samaria" in English could be translated as "watch mountain." Thus, we have another example of the tendency of imitation. The real "mountain" is the holy hill: "Yet have I set my king upon my holy hill of Zion" (Psalm 2:6). Samaria is not Zion but an imitation.

Warning to the Church

The tendency to promote the imitation is in full swing today in the church. We should not be surprised because Jesus warned: "Take heed that no man deceive you." De-

123

ception is believing in the fake, departing from the true way. It will ultimately lead to accepting Antichrist instead of Christ. Those who follow the wrong way will fall under the condemnation of 2 Thessalonians 2:11: "And for this cause God shall send them strong delusion, that they should believe a lie."

Chapter 14

Introduction

With chapter 14, we are concluding our study of the prophetic book of Hosea. This book and the book of Amos, as well as much of the book of Micah, are primarily directed against the ten-tribe rebellious Israel. But as we have mentioned several times during our study, these prophetic utterances are not singularly directed toward ten-tribe Israel; they include the kingdom of Judah and the Gentile world as well.

Hosea is the first book of the 12 Minor Prophets, and second only to Zechariah in content volume. But the message of both, and for that matter in all the books of prophecy, contains a strong warning, and an invitation to repent.

The book of Hosea gives us a revelation of God's unspeakable grace, expressed with the words in chapter 14, verse 4, "I will heal their backsliding, I will love them freely...."

Final Admonition to Repent

Hosea 14:1-2: "O Israel, return unto the LORD thy God; for thou hast fallen by thine iniquity. 2 Take with you words, and turn to the LORD: say unto him, Take away all iniquity, and receive us graciously: so will we render the calves of our lips."

(See) 1 Samuel 7:3-4; Psalm 51:16-17; Isaiah 55:6-7; Joel 2:13;
Micah 7:18-19; Romans 8:26; Hebrews 13:15

This indicates true repentance. No more relying on the sacrifice of bulls and goats, but rather our confession of faith with our lips.

Hosea 14:3: "Asshur shall not save us; we will not ride upon horses: neither will we say any more to the work of our hands, Ye are our gods: for in thee the fatherless findeth mercy."

(See) Psalm 10:14; 33:17; 68:5; Isaiah 31:1

The remnant of the ten-tribe Israel recognized that nothing will help; no military power, nor the idols they had worshiped in the past. The *Tanakh* reads, "...Nor ever again will we call our handiwork our god, since in you alone orphans find pity."

Modern Idols

If only we would take to heart this important warning and cease the worshiping of "idols" in our modern time. Of course, these are not the idols we see in museums and history books; our idols are our possessions, our achievements, our nation, and particularly our military, which is virtually worshiped these days. It is time to search our heart, for the Holy Spirit still convicts, and there is still time for repentance. When we face a Holy God, absolutely nothing is of any significance; in plain words, all is vanity.

126

Paul's Testimony

The great apostle Paul indeed had multiple reasons to be proud of himself, to trust in the flesh. He documents in Philippians 3:4-5 the following: "...If any other man thinketh that he hath whereof he might trust in the flesh, I more: Circumcised the eighth day, of the stock of Israel, of the tribe of Benjamin, an Hebrew of the Hebrews; as touching the law, a Pharisee." Israel is the nation above all other nations in the world. Paul comes from the tribe of Benjamin, the first tribe to be integrated into the tribe of Judah. He is a Hebrew, the people to whom God spoke. He was proud to be a Pharisee (although they are negatively presented in the New Testament). I don't think there are many of us who could say as Paul did, "touching the righteousness which is in the law, blameless." But what is his final conclusion about his nation, his heritage, his culture and religious standing? "Yea doubtless, and I count all things but loss for the excellency of the knowledge of Christ Jesus my Lord: for whom I have suffered the loss of all things, and do count them but dung, that I may win Christ" (verse 8). When compared with the knowledge of Christ, he counts them "but dung."

Only recognition of one's own corruptness will lead to the gate of grace.

God Will Heal

Hosea 14:4-7: "I will heal their backsliding, I will love them freely: for mine anger is turned away from him. 5 I will be as the dew unto Israel: he shall grow as the lily, and cast forth his roots as Lebanon. 6 His branches shall spread, and his beauty shall be as the olive tree, and his smell as Lebanon. 7 They that dwell under his shadow shall return; they shall revive as the corn, and grow as the vine: the scent thereof shall be as the wine of Lebanon."

(See) Proverbs 19:12; Song of Solomon 4:11; Isaiah 12:1; 26:19; 35:2; 57:18; Jeremiah 11:16

God's grace will break through and become effective when we humble ourselves, recognize our failure, and cast ourselves on the mercy of the God of Israel.

True Repentance

Hosea 14:8: "Ephraim shall say, What have I to do any more with idols? I have heard him, and observed him: I am like a green fir tree. From me is thy fruit found."

(See) Job 34:22; Isaiah 41:19; Ezekiel 17:23

This speaks of the remnant of Ephraim—Israel. The few, the true believers rejected idols and decisively turned to the Lord.

Finally, the book of Hosea concludes with two questions and three answers:

Hosea 14:9: "Who is wise, and he shall understand these things? prudent, and he shall know them? for the ways of the LORD are right, and the just shall walk in them: but the transgressors shall fall therein."

(See) Psalm 107:43; 111:7-8; Proverbs 10:29; Isaiah 1:28; 26:7;
Jeremiah 9:12; Zephaniah 3:5; John 18:37; Matthew 11:19

Job explains: "Behold, the fear of the Lord, that is wisdom; and to depart from evil is understanding" (Job 28:28). Job is the type of wisdom we need in these times, in order to distinguish between the way of the Lord and the way of the transgressors. Granted, this may sometimes be difficult to determine, but only to the extent that I have surrendered myself totally and unconditionally to the will of God, will I be able to fully and confidentially recognize the way of the Lord.

The rebellious, ten-tribe Israel has been rejected by the Lord as a separate identity from the tribe of Judah. But the remnant that joined themselves to the true God, under the umbrella of the tribe of Judah, became Jews and were integrated into the royal tribe. This is valid until this day: only Jews are granted the right to return to the land of Israel and become citizens of the State of Israel at arrival.

Conclusion

In conclusion, let us quote some Scriptures which clearly show that remnants of the ten rebellious tribes of Israel joined Judah: "For the Levites left their suburbs and their possession, and came to Judah and Jerusalem: for Jeroboam and his sons had cast them off from executing the priest's office unto the LORD...And after them out of all the tribes of Israel such as set their hearts to seek the LORD God of Israel came to Jerusalem, to sacrifice unto the LORD God of their fathers" (2 Chronicles

11:14, 16). "And he gathered all Judah and Benjamin, and the strangers with them out of Ephraim and Manasseh, and out of Simeon: for they fell to him out of Israel in abundance, when they saw that the LORD his God was with him" (2 Chronicles 15:9).

Although the kingdom of ten-tribe Israel ceased to exist, the individual members of each tribe kept their identity. In the final end, we see 12 tribes of the children of Israel, sealed during the Great Tribulation: "Of the tribe of Juda were sealed twelve thousand. Of the tribe of Reuben were sealed twelve thousand. Of the tribe of Gad were sealed twelve thousand. Of the tribe of Aser were sealed twelve thousand. Of the tribe of Nepthalim were sealed twelve thousand. Of the tribe of Manasses were sealed twelve thousand. Of the tribe of Simeon were sealed twelve thousand. Of the tribe of Levi were sealed twelve thousand. Of the tribe of Issachar were sealed twelve thousand. Of the tribe of Zabulon were sealed twelve thousand. Of the tribe of Joseph were sealed twelve thousand. Of the tribe of Benjamin were sealed twelve thousand" (Revelation 7:5-8).

Have you been integrated into the new nation, the holy nation? If yes, then the words of Ephesians 2:19 have been fulfilled in your life, "Now therefore ye are no more strangers and foreigners, but fellow citizens with the saints, and of the household of God."

AMOS
Burden Carrier

Chapter 9   215

The average reading time for the book of Amos is 21 minutes.

AMOS

Book of the Bible	God's Directly Spoken Words (%)	Prophecy %*	Significant Names Listed in Each Book						
			Judah	Israel	Ephraim	Jerusalem	Zion	Heathen	Samaria
Hosea	93.32	56	15	44	37	0	0	0	6
Joel	57.70	68	6	3	0	6	7	5	0
Amos	**80.95**	**58**	**4**	**30**	**0**	**2**	**2**	**1**	**5**
Obadiah	97.69	81	1	1	1	2	2	4	1
Jonah	7.39	10	0	0	0	0	0	0	0
Micah	44.88	70	4	12	0	8	9	1	3
Nahum	40.30	74	1	1	0	0	0	0	0
Habakkuk	47.84	41	0	0	0	0	0	2	0
Zephaniah	96.92	89	3	4	0	4	2	1	0
Haggai	67.61	39	4	0	0	0	0	1	0
Zechariah	77.38	69	22	5	3	41	8	5	0
Malachi	93.80	56	3	5	0	2	0	2	0

* Percentage of book as prophecy according to *Tim LaHaye Prophecy Study Bible*

Introduction to Amos

Among the prophets, Amos is unique because it starts with the words of Amos. In most cases, it says that the word of the Lord came to the prophet. Also unique is that "he saw concerning Israel."

The message is not limited to ten-tribe Israel, for we read the name "Judah" four times. Moreover, the Gentiles are not excluded from the devastating message of judgment.

Amos's prophecies conclude with the promise of God, "I will bring again the captivity of my people Israel." This speaks to the remnant of the 12 tribes: "…and they shall no more be pulled up out of their land which I have giveth them, saith the Lord thy God."

We include Amos in the category of "Prophecy for Ten-Tribe Israel," because Israel is mentioned thirty times, and Samaria five times. However, we will continue to emphasize that all the prophets are addressed to all people of all times, but on occasion specifically directed to a named group of people.

Chapter 1

Introduction

The first chapter is primarily directed against Israel's enemies, specifically five neighbors: Damascus, Gaza, Tyrus, Edom, and Ammon. The reason for the punishing judgment is revealed. The name Amos, meaning "burden," is key to the prophetic book.

Shepherd from Tekoa

Amos 1:1: "The words of Amos, who was among the herdmen of Tekoa, which he saw concerning Israel in the days of Uzziah king of Judah, and in the days of Jeroboam the son of Joash king of Israel, two years before the earthquake."

(See) 2 Samuel 14:2; 2 Chronicles 11:6; Psalm 78:70; Hosea 1:1;
Zechariah 14:5

Amos was a shepherd who lived in the desert of Tekoa, located south of Jerusalem. His task was most unusual in that he, coming from Judah, was sent to Israel to call attention to their sins against the God of Israel.

Unger's Bible Dictionary makes an interesting observation: "The two kingdoms were at the summit of their prosperity. Idleness, luxury, and oppression were general, and idolatry prevalent. It was at such a time as this that the plain shepherd of Tekoah was sent into Israel and prophesied at Beth-el. This is almost a solitary instance of a prophet being sent from Judah into Israel."

The Burden Carrier

Amos 1:2: "And he said, The LORD will roar from Zion, and utter his voice from Jerusalem; and the habitations of the shepherds shall mourn, and the top of Carmel shall wither."

(See) Jeremiah 12:4; 25:30; Joel 1:18-19; 3:16

Amos, meaning "burden," certainly describes his calling because Amos carried a great burden the Lord had placed upon him: to proclaim His message to Israel and the surrounding nations.

Amos identifies himself as a herdsman of Tekoa, and supplies us with the date by revealing that Uzziah was king of Judah and Jeroboam was king of Israel. A special event is also mentioned: "two years before the earthquake."

Judgment from Zion

The prophet announced impending judgment coming from Zion and Jerusalem. Obviously, this was not a pleasant message for anyone; it was the day of judgment from the Lord and, as a result, "the shepherds shall mourn, and the top of Carmel shall wither." No wonder Amaziah the priest ordered Amos to stop prophesying: "prophesy not again any more at Bethel: for it is the king's chapel, and it is the king's court" (Amos 7:13). In other words, "Leave us alone; we don't need your negative prophecies! Our ears are inclined to hear the more positive things in life."

Unpopular Prophecy

During my years of ministry in various countries, the question most often asked was: why is the prophetic Word not taught in our churches? The answer is simple: people have their own agendas. Those who are of retirement age look forward to the "golden years." The so-called middle-aged wait for their children to graduate from school, move out and start their own families. Adolescents dream of growing up, finishing school, landing a great job, getting married, and living happily ever after. Why would anyone want to listen to a message that warns of the coming doomsday, the judgment of God, the Day of the Lord?

Fortunately, however, there are a select few who have their minds anchored in God's Word. They have realized that whatever comes upon this earth does not affect their eternal security, because their feet are placed upon the solid Rock. They want to hear God's Word, spend more of their time reading the Bible. They are already rejoicing about that which is to come; namely, the fulfillment of John 14:3: "...I go and prepare a place for you, I will come again, and receive you unto myself; that where I am, there ye may be also."

Message to Israel's Neighbors

Before Amos addresses Israel, he proclaims judgment

against the surrounding nations: Syria, Gaza, Lebanon, Edom, Ammon and Moab.

It seems strange that he goes straight north to the city of Damascus in the land of Syria, then crosses southwest to Gaza, the land of the Philistines. Next he moves north again to Tyrus, the land of Lebanon. From there he crosses Israel to the land of Edom, located south of the Dead Sea. Then he heads north a third time, to the land of Ammon, and finally down south to the land of Moab, east of the Salt Sea.

Amos did not mention these countries in geographic succession, from left to right or clockwise, but he criss-crossed Israel to point to the sins of the neighboring countries.

I believe this has prophetic significance. As we have read, judgment will come from Jerusalem and Zion; that means it involves Israel each time. This also reveals Israel's failure as a nation to be a light unto the Gentiles. In other words, Israel was connected to the failure of the neighboring nations.

Israel's Calling Not Fulfilled

We must recall what Moses said about Israel: "For thou art an holy people unto the LORD thy God: the LORD thy God hath chosen thee to be a special people unto himself, above all people that are upon the face of the earth" (Deuteronomy 7:6). Furthermore, we read in Deuteronomy 15:6, "For the LORD thy God blesseth thee, as he promised thee: and thou shalt lend unto many nations, but thou shalt not borrow; and thou shalt reign over many nations, but they shall not reign over thee."

143

These and many other promises could not be fulfilled at that time because of disobedience.

God's commandment was clear: they were to get rid of all the inhabitants of the Promised Land, from the river of Egypt to the Euphrates River. But they did not follow all of God's instructions.

Israel-Judah and Ten-Tribe Israel

During Amos' time, Israel existed as an independent nation, although in two parts: 1) Israel-Judah; and 2) the ten-tribe Israel. It is important to realize that God chose Judah as the tribe for Israel to find their identity in. Judah did not rebel against the ten-tribe Israel, but the 10 tribes rebelled against Judah: "So Israel rebelled against the house of David unto this day" (1 Kings 12:19).

The Holy Spirit inspired Amos to bring a message of judgment first to the surrounding nations.

Damascus

Amos 1:3-5: "Thus saith the LORD; For three transgressions of Damascus, and for four, I will not turn away the punishment thereof; because they have threshed Gilead with threshing instruments of iron: 4 But I will send a fire into the house of Hazael, which shall devour the palaces of Benhadad. 5 I will break also the bar of Damascus, and cut off the inhabitant from the plain of Aven, and him that holdeth the sceptre from the house of Eden: and the people of Syria shall go into captivity unto Kir, saith the LORD."

(See) 2 Kings 10:32-33; 16:9; Isaiah 8:4; Lamentations 2:9

What does "for three transgressions of Damascus, and for four" mean? It meant that Damascus would not be punished because of three or four sins, but because of the sins they committed against Gilead. In the same manner, he pronounced judgment upon Gaza, Tyrus, Edom, Ammon and Moab. In other words, God was saying in effect, "When I judge Israel, I will also judge you!"

The Transgression of Damascus
The prophet used only ten words to identify Damascus' transgression, "because they have threshed Gilead with threshing instruments of iron." Damascus transgressed the fundamental principles God had ordained relating to war and the handling of enemies.

We find a clue in 2 Kings 8:12: "And Hazael said, Why weepeth my lord? And he answered, Because I know the evil that thou wilt do unto the children of Israel: their strong holds wilt thou set on fire, and their young men wilt thou slay with the sword, and wilt dash their children, and rip up their women with child." This most horrible thing was even incomprehensible to Hazael himself. He actually protested against this prophecy in the next verse: "And Hazael said, But what, is thy servant a dog, that he should do this great thing?"

The Sin of Gaza

Amos 1:6-8: "Thus saith the LORD: For three transgressions of Gaza, and for four, I will not turn away the punishment thereof; because they carried away captive the whole captivity, to deliver them up to Edom: 7 But I will send a fire on the wall of Gaza, which shall devour the palaces thereof: 8 And I will cut off the inhabitant from Ashdod, and him that holdeth the sceptre from Ashkelon, and I will turn mine hand against Ekron: and the remnant of the Philistines shall perish, saith the Lord GOD."

(See) 2 Kings 18:8; 2 Chronicles 28:18

Why was Gaza punished? "Because they carried away captive the whole captivity, to deliver them up to Edom." Taking an enemy captive was their legal right. But the issue here is that they took captives and did not use them as servants to work in their fields, build their houses and tend to the animals; they delivered them to Edom. That's about 120 kilometers to the east. Gaza's sin was making merchandise of man when they sold them to Edom.

Therefore, Gaza comes under the fiery judgment of God, including Ashdod, Ashkelon and Ekron, the southwest territory of the Promised Land.

It is interesting that Gaza is quite often mentioned in the news media. Even today, they are sending "fire," rockets and missiles against Israel, and in return receive severe punishment of firepower by Israel's defense forces.

The Sin of Tyrus

Amos 1:9-10: "Thus saith the LORD; For three transgressions of Tyrus, and for four, I will not turn away the punishment thereof; because they delivered up the whole captivity to Edom, and remembered not the brotherly covenant: 10 But I will send a fire on the wall of Tyrus, which shall devour the palaces thereof."

(See) Ezekiel 26:2-4; Joel 3:4-8

The reason for the punishment is the same as that of Gaza, "because they delivered up the whole captivity to Edom." That was one thing, but then it continues, "and remembered not the brotherly covenant." This goes back to the time of David. Read 2 Samuel 5:11: "And Hiram king of Tyre sent messengers to David, and cedar trees, and carpenters, and masons: and they built David an house." The Bible calls it "the brotherly covenant." Here in Amos we see this historical covenant of friendship between David and the king of Lebanon violated.

The Sin of Edom

Amos 1:11-12: "Thus saith the LORD; For three transgressions of Edom, and for four, I will not turn away the punishment thereof; because he did pursue his brother with the sword, and did cast off all pity, and his anger did tear perpetually, and he kept his wrath for ever: 12 But I will send a fire upon Teman, which shall devour the palaces of Bozrah."

(See) Malachi 1:4

Their transgression is identified with the words, "he did

pursue his brother with the sword...and his anger did tear perpetually, and he kept his wrath for ever."

Edom is Esau, the brother of Jacob. Esau was an evil person; he hated his brother Jacob. In Genesis 27:41 we read, "...and Esau said in his heart, The days of mourning for my father are at hand; then will I slay my brother Jacob." That sin was never repented of and remained with Edom.

For Israel, the commandment was given not to hate: "Thou shalt not abhor an Edomite; for he is thy brother: thou shalt not abhor an Egyptian; because thou wast a stranger in his land" (Deuteronomy 23:7).

The Sin of Ammon

Amos 1:13-15: "Thus saith the LORD; For three transgressions of the children of Ammon, and for four, I will not turn away the punishment thereof; because they have ripped up the women with child of Gilead, that they might enlarge their border: 14 But I will kindle a fire in the wall of Rabbah, and it shall devour the palaces thereof, with shouting in the day of battle, with a tempest in the day of the whirlwind: 15 And their king shall go into captivity, he and his princes together, saith the LORD."

(See) Deuteronomy 3:11; Jeremiah 49:2-3; Ezekiel 25:5

What was Ammon's sin? "...they have ripped up the women with child of Gilead, that they might enlarge their border." They practiced extreme cruelty with a specific aim: "that they might enlarge their border."

Almost 200 years later, about 600 B.C., we hear the prophet Jeremiah asking questions about the territory of the Ammonites: "Concerning the Ammonites, thus saith the LORD; Hath Israel no sons? hath he no heir? why then doth their king inherit Gad, and his people dwell in his cities?" (Jeremiah 49:1).

The Church

We are in a parallel position today when we compare the Church with the world. There is no question that judgment will come upon the world; that has already been determined in prophetic Scripture. It will come to pass. The Great Tribulation will be the most horrible event ever to take place upon planet Earth.

One must realize the condition of the world before judgment: "How much she hath glorified herself, and lived deliciously, so much torment and sorrow give her: for she saith in her heart, I sit a queen, and am no widow, and shall see no sorrow" (Revelation 18:7). That's a description of extreme prosperity. This refers to Mystery Babylon, the economic, political, financial and religious system of the world. All will be destroyed by God's judgment.

Revelation 3:17 speaks of the end time church (Laodicea). Their own testimony reveals their prosperity: "I am rich, and increased with goods, and have need of nothing." However, the difference between the judgment of the Church and the judgment of the world is that the Church will be judged unto salvation. Believers will appear before Christ: "For we must all appear before the judgment seat of Christ; that every one may receive the things done in his body, according to that he hath done, whether it be good or bad" (2 Corinthians 5:10). This is the reward-judgment. This has no relationship to condemnation. The issue of salvation has been settled; it does not depend on our work, but on the already accomplished work of Jesus Christ on the cross.

It may be helpful to read 1 Corinthians 3:14-15: "If any man's work abide which he hath built thereupon, he shall receive a reward. If any man's work shall be burned, he shall suffer loss: but he himself shall be saved; yet so as by fire."

The destiny of the Church is described in Revelation 19:7-8: "Let us be glad and rejoice, and give honour to him: for the marriage of the Lamb is come, and his wife hath made herself ready. And to her was granted that she should be arrayed in fine linen, clean and white: for the fine linen is the righteousness of saints."

The destiny of the nations that rebel against the God of heaven is described in Revelation 20:14-15: "And death and hell were cast into the lake of fire. This is the second death. And whosoever was not found written in the book of life was cast into the lake of fire."

Chapter 2

Introduction

God's wrath continues upon Moab and Judah, but most of the chapter concerns Israel. The conclusion is the revelation of Israel's military downfall.

The Sin of Moab

Amos 2:1-3: "Thus saith the LORD; For three transgressions of Moab, and for four, I will not turn away the punishment thereof; because he burned the bones of the king of Edom into lime: 2 But I will send a fire upon Moab, and it shall devour the palaces of Kirioth: and Moab shall die with tumult, with shouting, and with the sound of the trumpet: 3 And I will cut off the judge from the midst thereof, and will slay all the princes thereof with him, saith the LORD."

(See) Numbers 24:17; 2 Kings 3:27; Jeremiah 48:41; Ezekiel 25:8; Zephaniah 2:8

The accusation is revealed with the words, "because he burned the bones of the king of Edom into lime." That was a violation against God's fundamental law relating to the disposal of a body.

To the first man, Adam, after he had transgressed, God said, "For dust thou art, and unto dust shalt thou return." The burning of a body or bones always indicated

151

judgment, and was never practiced in the Bible by those who followed God.

This Scripture clearly expresses the opposition to the increasingly popular way of disposing a body: cremation. It is interesting that when some clergy officiate a funeral they not only say, "Dust to dust," but add "ashes to ashes," which is not found in Holy Scripture.

Furthermore, it is God who installs kings, even in enemy lands, and the Moabites disregarded that fact. Besides, the King of Moab committed a further abomination by sacrificing his own son by fire, as recorded in 2 Kings 3:27: "Then he took his eldest son that should have reigned in his stead, and offered him for a burnt offering upon the wall. And there was great indignation against Israel: and they departed from him, and returned to their own land."

The Transgression of Judah

Amos 2:4-5: "Thus saith the LORD; For three transgressions of Judah, and for four, I will not turn away the punishment thereof; because they have despised the law of the LORD, and have not kept his commandments, and their lies caused them to err, after the which their fathers have walked: 5 I will send a fire upon Judah, and it shall devour the palaces of Jerusalem."

(See) Nehemiah 1:7; Isaiah 5:24; 28:15; Jeremiah 16:19; Ezekiel 20:13, 16; Daniel 9:11; Hosea 8:14

A similar judgment was pronounced upon Tyrus and

Edom, and in most cases it was because of their mistreatment of their brother. We note that Judas' guilt is identified in their despising the law of God: "because they have despised the law of the Lord, and have not kept his commandments."

Judah, according to the prophecies of Jacob, was to be "the lawgiver." From his line the Messiah would come: "…unto him shall the gathering of the people be" (Genesis 49:10).

The geographic location of Jerusalem is significant: it is the place where in the fullness of time, Jesus fulfilled the commandments of the law by sacrificing Himself on Calvary's Cross. From Jerusalem, the Lord's voice will be uttered, the voice of judgment upon Judah, Jerusalem and the entire world.

Judah despised the law of the Lord. That is a terrible thing. The "lawgiver" despises the law, which is all but unthinkable. This shows that in the heart of man, there is no good. When one despises God's Word, it is but natural to ignore His commandments.

The basic principles laid out in the Ten Commandments, given to the people of Israel, are the foundation for all civilized nations in the world, regardless of their religion or non-religion. But Judah the "Lawgiver" failed to keep the law. The words, "And their lies caused them to err," show that when we do not take heed of the Word of God, we despise God. Jesus summarized the entire law in Matthew 22:38-40, "This is the first and great commandment. And the second is like unto it, Thou shalt love thy neighbour as thyself. On these two commandments hang all the law and the prophets."

Whenever we deviate from such fundamental truths, we will be led astray into a false teaching, into a lie. That is what happened to Judah.

The Transgression of Israel

After pronouncing judgment upon the six neighboring nations and upon Judah, the prophet turns to ten-tribe Israel:

Amos 2:6-8: "Thus saith the LORD; For three transgressions of Israel, and for four, I will not turn away the punishment thereof; because they sold the righteous for silver, and the poor for a pair of shoes; 7 That pant after the dust of the earth on the head of the poor, and turn aside the way of the meek: and a man and his father will go in unto the same maid, to profane my holy name: 8 And they lay themselves down upon clothes laid to pledge by every altar, and they drink the wine of the condemned in the house of their god."

(See) Leviticus 20:3; Isaiah 10:2; 29:21; Ezekiel 22:11; 36:20; Romans 2:24

A seven-fold sin is exposed:

1."Because they sold the righteous for silver...." Isaiah 10:2 explains: "To turn aside the needy from judgment, and to take away the right from the poor of my people, that widows may be their prey, and that they may rob the fatherless!"

2."...And the poor for a pair of shoes." Later in Amos 8:6 it says: "That we may buy the poor for silver, and the needy for a pair of shoes; yea, and sell the refuse of the wheat?"

3."That pant after the dust of the earth on the head of the poor...." Israel oppressed the poor, yet throughout Scripture they were instructed to support the poor. The New Testament too admonishes us: "Remember the poor" (Galatians 2:10).

4."...And turn aside the way of the meek...." Yet the promise is given to the meek: "The meek will he guide in judgment: and the meek will he teach his way" (Psalm 25:9).

5."...And a man and his father will go in unto the same maid, to profane my holy name." Although prostitution was part of the culture of society at that time, the case mentioned here was one of the most horrible abominations and punishable with death. In the New Testament we read in 1 Corinthians 5:1: "It is reported commonly that there is fornication among you, and such fornication as is not so much as named among the Gentiles, that one should have his father's wife." The Apostle Paul had the authority to execute judgment, as we read in verse 5: "To deliver such an one unto Satan for the destruction of the flesh, that the spirit may be saved in the day of the Lord Jesus."

6."...They lay themselves down upon clothes laid to pledge by every altar...." Exodus 22:26 reads: "If thou at all take thy neighbour's raiment to pledge, thou shalt deliver it unto him by that the sun goeth down." The garment of a person was very personal and had to be returned before the sun sets. But here Israel uses the garment as bedding, and made it an idol altar!

7."...and they drink the wine of the condemned in the house of their god." The *Tanakh* clarifies this with the following words: "And drink in the House of their God wine bought with fines they imposed."

We notice that the enumeration of sins committed by Israel against God is carefully detailed. These are the people who should have known better, yet they openly, deliberately and intentionally violated the laws God had given to them through the prophet Moses.

Amorite Example

To illustrate God's displeasure with His people Israel, He gives as example the Amorites, who occupied part of the Promised Land before Israel came to take possession thereof.

Amos 2:9-11: "Yet destroyed I the Amorite before them, whose height was like the height of the cedars, and he was strong as the oaks; yet I destroyed his fruit from above, and his roots from beneath. 10 Also I brought you up from the land of Egypt, and led you forty years through the wilderness, to possess the land of the Amorite. 11 And I raised up of your sons for prophets, and of your young men for Nazarites. Is it not even thus, O ye children of Israel? saith the LORD."

(See) Judges 13:5

How did Israel react?

Amos 2:12: "But ye gave the Nazarites wine to drink; and commanded the prophets, saying, Prophesy not."

(See) Isaiah 30:10; Acts 4:18

156

Israel was acting diametrically opposed to God's instruction, "Prophesy not."

This is typical for our days as well. In an age of peace and prosperity, who wants to hear about judgment, destruction and punishment? Thus, the Church at large deliberately rejects the prophetic Word today.

We note that the Israelites were well-off, living in peace and luxury. As a result, they ignored and rejected the Word of God, even forbidding the proclamation of the prophetic Word.

Our Days Prophetically

It is noteworthy that ministries, churches and preachers who proclaim the positive gospel, who promise health, wealth and happiness, are the most successful these days. That is quite natural. Everyone has their own plans; thus, the prophetic plan does not correspond to our self-made plans. By nature, we are overemphasizing our needs here and now above the real need—taking note of the prophetic Word.

Jesus mentions the normal day-to-day activity that took place during the times of Noah and Lot in Luke 17:26-29: "And as it was in the days of Noe, so shall it be also in the days of the Son of man. They did eat, they drank, they married wives, they were given in marriage, until the day that Noe entered into the ark, and the flood came, and destroyed them all. Likewise also as it was in the days of Lot; they did eat, they drank, they bought, they sold, they planted, they builded; But the same day that Lot went out of Sodom it rained fire and brimstone from heaven, and destroyed them all." No mention is made of the sin of Sodom and Gomorrah, nor the disregard for Noah's warning. Jesus enumerates normal things we do today. But in the midst of the normal activity, there should be one priority: seeking the Lord and His will, as revealed by the prophetic Word.

The proclamation of the prophetic Word will continue to decrease. We are living in the "now generation." Success is manifested through the avenue of self-elevation, self-proclamation, self-gratification and self-esteem!

An Eightfold Judgment

Instead of the glorious future Israel was expecting, God pronounced an eight-fold judgment:

Amos 2:13-16: "Behold, I am pressed under you, as a cart is pressed that is full of sheaves. 14 Therefore the flight shall perish from the swift, and the strong shall not strengthen his force, neither shall the mighty deliver himself: 15 Neither shall he stand that handleth the bow; and he that is swift of foot shall not deliver himself: neither shall he that rideth the horse deliver himself. 16 And he that is courageous among the mighty shall flee away naked in that day, saith the LORD."

(See) Psalm 33:16; Isaiah 30:16-17; 31:3; Jeremiah 9:23; 51:56

"Behold, I am pressed under you, as a cart is pressed that is full of sheaves." The *Tanakh* reads: "Ah, I will slow your movements as a wagon is slowed when it is full of cut grain" (verse 13).

When we read the words, "full of sheaves...swift...strong...force...mighty...the bow...rideth the horse...courageous...mighty," it is evident that Israel was prosperous and well established; the barns were full, the mighty were strong. They had everything but it would not help in the end, because Israel worshiped success instead of realizing it was due to God's blessing.

The End Time Days

What a tremendous prophecy for our days. Reliance on God the Creator has virtually disappeared from the public at large. Simple, childlike faith in the living God has been replaced with man's achievement. The guideline for the day is not prayer but news about the various stock exchanges around the globe, proclaimed 24 hours a day. Financial movements, commerce, productivity, and profits have become the god of this world.

We must emphasize here there is little, if any, difference between the so-called Christian nations, the Buddhists, the Hindus, the Muslims, and the atheists. Speaking of atheism, the official philosophy of communism, China has become the "savior" of the world with their immense cash resources.

Our times are clearly marked by the accumulation of riches and prosperity: possessions are the goal of humanity.

Chapter 3

Introduction

Several extraordinary things are revealed in this chapter. First, God has not chosen any other nation but Israel, "You only have I known of all the families of the earth." Second, the sovereignty of God is revealed with the words, "Shall there be evil in a city, and the Lord hath not done it?" The last verse reveals utter devastation of Israel's prosperity.

Judgment against Israel

Amos 3:1-2: "Hear this word that the LORD hath spoken against you, O children of Israel, against the whole family which I brought up from the land of Egypt, saying, 2 You only have I known of all the families of the earth: therefore I will punish you for all your iniquities."

(See) Jeremiah 13:11; 14:10; Ezekiel 20:36

The announcement of judgment against Israel was directed primarily toward the ten-tribe Israel, the one that rebelled against Judah. Nevertheless, the introduction includes all of Israel, "against the whole family which I brought up from the land of Egypt" (verse 1). Therefore, this message applies to all 12 tribes. They all are from one family, the family God chose for His predetermined plan to bring forth the Redeemer, the Messiah of Israel, the Savior for the world.

We also note the words, "all the families of the earth." Thus, judgment is directed against Israel, Judah and the world.

Seven Questions

Then the prophet asked seven questions:

Amos 3:3-6: "Can two walk together, except they be agreed? 4 Will a lion roar in the forest, when he hath no prey? will a young lion cry out of his den, if he have taken nothing? 5 Can a bird fall in a snare upon the earth, where no gin is for him? shall one take up a snare from the earth, and have taken nothing at all? 6 Shall a trumpet be blown in the city, and the people not be afraid? shall there be evil in a city, and the LORD hath not done it?"

(See) Psalm 104:21; Jeremiah 4:5, 19

These questions demonstrate God's absolute sovereignty over all things. Just as it is impossible for a bird to fall into a trap when there is no bait, it is impossible for anything—good or bad—to be out of the Lord's power.

Moses testified of God's sovereignty: "See now that I, even I, am he, and there is no god with me: I kill, and I make alive; I wound, and I heal: neither is there any that can deliver out of my hand" (Deuteronomy 32:39). Furthermore, the prophet Isaiah wrote: "I form the light, and create darkness: I make peace, and create evil: I the LORD do all these things" (Isaiah 45:7).

161

God is in absolute control. He chose Israel; He brought them from out of the land of Egypt, and He will now execute punishment for their iniquities.

With these questions, God also confirms the necessity of judgment against Israel. He will make it known to His people by His prophets:

Amos 3:7-8: "Surely the Lord GOD will do nothing, but he revealeth his secret unto his servants the prophets. 8 The lion hath roared, who will not fear? the Lord GOD hath spoken, who can but prophesy?"

(See) Genesis 6:13; Proverbs 3:32; Daniel 9:22-27; John 15:15;
Revelation 1:1, 19

The prophet made sure that the people who heard his words understood the irreversible pronouncement of judgment. Just as the roaring of a lion causes fear, so will the words of the prophet.

The Heathen Shall Bear Witness

Amos 3:9-10: "Publish in the palaces at Ashdod, and in the palaces in the land of Egypt, and say, Assemble yourselves upon the mountains of Samaria, and behold the great tumults in the midst thereof, and the oppressed in the midst thereof. 10 For they know not to do right, saith the LORD, who store up violence and robbery in their palaces."

(See) 1 Samuel 5:1; Psalm 14:4; Jeremiah 4:22

162

Ashdod and Egypt are invited to witness Israel's sins. Israel has become incapable of doing what is right. We must realize that these accusations against Israel are extremely serious, because of their special position. God said: "You only have I known of all the families of the earth." The Lord knows Israel. They are God's chosen people, yet they failed.

"I Never Knew You"

In Matthew 7, the Lord Jesus speaks to a group of "believers" He did not "know." They testify: "Lord, Lord, have we not prophesied in thy name? and in thy name have cast out devils? and in thy name done many wonderful works?" (verse 22). They list their activities, their dedicated works, but still Jesus said, "I never knew you: depart from me, ye that work iniquity." Why didn't Jesus recognize them? Because these people had not produced any true fruits of righteousness. These "religious" people were rejected; they remained *unknown* to the Lord.

Arabs in the Promised Land

Amos 3:11: "Therefore thus saith the Lord GOD; An adversary there shall be even round about the land; and he shall bring down thy strength from thee, and thy palaces shall be spoiled."

(See) 2 King 17:6

Israel did become powerless and desolate, and was "spoiled." Even today, Samaria, called the "West Bank,"

163

is being trodden down by Arab-Palestinians; it is occupied by foreigners. It is also significant that the whole world agrees that the Arab-Palestinians should take possession of Judea and Samaria.

However, we must add that this is temporary, because God's sovereignty is not reliant upon what the nations do or don't do. At this time, He permits Israel's enemies, with the support of the entire world, to bring this evil upon the Promised Land, fulfilling His Word, "Shall there be evil in a city, and the Lord hath not done it?"

A Glimmer of Hope

Then comes a little spark of hope:

Amos 3:12: "Thus saith the LORD; As the shepherd taketh out of the mouth of the lion two legs, or a piece of an ear; so shall the children of Israel be taken out that dwell in Samaria in the corner of a bed, and in Damascus in a couch."

(See) 1 Samuel 17:34-37; Esther 1:6; 7:8; Psalm 132:8

Although this may not be much, it's better than nothing. The ten-tribe Israel has been devoured by the enemy, but there remain remnants, "two legs, or a piece of an ear." That means the "two legs" can run to escape the ultimate destruction, and the "piece of an ear" surely reminds us of their ability to hear. As a matter of fact, that is how chapter 3 of the book of Amos begins: "Hear this word...O children of Israel."

Only a tiny remnant was left; that remnant was added

to Judah/Israel. This took place long before the ultimate destruction of the ten-tribe Israel.

Almost 200 years before the event described by Amos, remnants of the tribes of Israel refused to worship the golden calves of Samaria. Jeroboam, the king of Israel, "ordained him priests for the high places, and for the devils, and for the calves which he had made...," but there was a remnant, "...out of all the tribes of Israel such as set their hearts to seek the LORD God of Israel came to Jerusalem, to sacrifice unto the LORD God of their fathers" (2 Chronicles 11:15-16). Note, however, they have no more identity as an individual kingdom. The ten-tribe Israel was *devoured*; only the remnant escaped. The ten-tribe Israel was incorporated into the tribe of Judah and became Jews, as they are known today. Yet the time will come when the 12 tribes of Israel are identified and reestablished in accordance with Ezekiel chapter 48.

The Remnant Church

For the Church, chapter 3 contains an extremely serious message. The Church of Jesus Christ is not a visible identity on the earth. The Church, made up of born-again Christians, is the *remnant* of believers from all over the world. They believe the Word of God, reverently fear it, tremble at His message, pray on bended knee, and proclaim that judgment is coming upon planet Earth. These believers may only be few in number, but they can be found in all four corners of the earth.

The Apostle Paul identified these people in Ephesians 2:19: "Now therefore ye are no more strangers and foreigners, but fellowcitizens with the saints, and of the household of God." We belong to Israel, the only family known to God. We must not cave in under these seemingly discouraging circumstances that we witness daily, but we must hold ourselves to the invisible Lord, who has given us His Word. That is our only guideline from now until eternity begins at the moment of the Rapture, or our physical death.

The End of the Altar of Bethel

Judgment upon the ten-tribe Israel was executed to the fullest extent:

> **Amos 3:13-15:** "Hear ye, and testify in the house of Jacob, saith the Lord GOD, the God of hosts, 14 That in the day that I shall visit the transgressions of Israel upon him I will also visit the altars of Bethel: and the horns of the altar shall be cut off, and fall to the ground. 15 And I will smite the winter house with the summer house; and the houses of ivory shall perish, and the great houses shall have an end, saith the LORD."

(See) 1 Kings 22:39; 2 Kings 23:15; Jeremiah 36:22; Ezekiel 2:7

Not only are the physical houses and palaces gone, but the ten-tribe house of Israel perished and "shall have an end, saith the Lord."

Bible prophecy fulfillment is being disregarded by Churchianity, yet Scripture admonishes us to "hear this word that the Lord hath spoken."

Remember, our political identities have no future. Na-

166

tionalities are temporary; all are destined to be invali-
dated. But he who has his identity established in the family of God, the household of the saints, is building on the
solid foundation and will not perish.

Chapter 4

Introduction

God's relentless exposure of Israel's sin highlights their practice of idolatry, oppression, and stubbornness. His burning anger is expressed with the words, "Prepare to meet thy God, O Israel."

The "Kine of Bashan"

Amos 4:1: "Hear this word, ye kine of Bashan, that are in the mountain of Samaria, which oppress the poor, which crush the needy, which say to their masters, Bring, and let us drink."

(See) Psalm 22:12; Ezekiel 39:18

In chapters one and two, we learned how the Lord spoke against Damascus, Gaza, Tyrus, Edom, Ammon, Moab, Judah and Israel. And at the beginning of chapter 3, it very clearly said, "Hear this word that the Lord hath spoken against you, O children of Israel...."

Now we read, "Hear this word, ye kine of Bashan." Who are the "kine of Bashan"? Is God speaking to the cattle on the mountains of Samaria? Quite obviously, that is not the case because these "kine of Bashan" committed sins animals are not capable of, "oppress the poor...crush the needy...." They are violating the fundamental principles that God has entrusted to Israel, and through Israel to the entire world; namely, compassion on the poor and support of the needy.

There is one other clue as to their identity: the words, "which say to their masters." The German Menge translation actually says, "they which say to their husbands." This points to the fact that the "kine of Bashan" refers to the ladies of Samaria.

We know from Biblical history that Bashan was a very fertile area and produced excellent cattle. These rich ladies from the house of Israel were apparently well off, living in luxury at the cost of the poor and downtrodden. Now they invite their husbands, "Let us drink." Why are these women called the "kine of Bashan"? Because of their animalistic behavior. That's one reason the antichrist is called the *beast*—because of his total and absolute disregard for God.

Man consists of spirit, soul and body, while animal consists of soul and body only. An animal has a brain but no spirit; thus, the behavior of mankind, dedicating himself to idolatry, became animalistic.

The Golden Calf

Even before Israel entered the Promised Land, they rebelled against the living God at the time when Moses went up on the mountain to receive the commandments. What was the manifestation of their rebellion? "And all the people brake off the golden earrings which were in their ears, and brought them unto Aaron. And he received them at their hand, and fashioned it with a graving tool, after he had made it a molten calf: and they said, These be thy gods, O Israel, which brought thee up

169

out of the land of Egypt" (Exodus 32:3-4). Israel, chosen by God, is now stupefied to such an extent that they manufacture an animal, a golden calf, which becomes their god; thus, Israel became animalistic.

What next? "And when Aaron saw it, he built an altar before it; and Aaron made proclamation, and said, To-morrow is a feast to the LORD. And they rose up early on the morrow, and offered burnt offerings, and brought peace offerings; and the people sat down to eat and to drink, and rose up to play" (Exodus 32:5-6). Israel, the holy people of God, threw themselves into indulgences of unimaginable magnitude, gratifying the lusts of the flesh in an animalistic fashion.

The End Is at Hand

How does God answer the animalistic behavior of these ladies, the "kine of Bashan"?

Amos 4:2-3: "The Lord GOD hath sworn by his holiness, that, lo, the days shall come upon you, that he will take you away with hooks, and your posterity with fishhooks. 3 And ye shall go out at the breaches, every cow at that which is before her; and ye shall cast them into the palace, saith the LORD."

(See) Psalm 89:35; Isaiah 37:29; Jeremiah 16:16; Ezekiel 29:4; 38:4

Again, he is speaking against the "kine of Bashan." Yet, it is the end of ten-tribe Israel as a separate entity from the royal tribe, Judah-Israel.

The next two verses express Israel's hopelessness from

God's perspective:

Amos 4:4-5: "Come to Bethel, and transgress; at Gilgal multiply transgression; and bring your sacrifices every morning, and your tithes after three years: 5 And offer a sacrifice of thanksgiving with leaven, and proclaim and publish the free offerings: for this liketh you, O ye children of Israel, saith the Lord GOD."

(See) Numbers 28:3-4; Deuteronomy 12:6; Ezekiel 20:39; Hosea 4:15

In other words, do as you please; violate all the principles and laws laid out in the Scripture; disregard God's clear instruction; ignore the living God of Israel. Why? Because for you, there is no more hope.

Failure to Repent
God, through His prophet reminds them that He did send punishment upon Israel, but without result:

Amos 4:6: "And I also have given you cleanness of teeth in all your cities, and want of bread in all your places: yet have ye not returned unto me, saith the LORD."

(See) 1 Kings 17:1; Isaiah 3:1; 9:13; Jeremiah 5:3; Hosea 5:15; Haggai 2:17

Famine did not turn Israel to repentance; they did not seek the Lord.

Amos 4:7-8: "And also I have withholden the rain from you, when there were yet three months to the harvest:

and I caused it to rain upon one city, and caused it not to rain upon another city: one piece was rained upon, and the piece whereupon it rained not withered. 8 So two or three cities wandered unto one city, to drink water; but they were not satisfied: yet have ye not returned unto me, saith the LORD."

(See) Deuteronomy 11:17; 1 Kings 18:5; Jeremiah 3:7; 14:4

The Lord God withheld rain, and when rain did fall, it was very selective. But the result was negative: "Yet have ye not returned unto me, saith the Lord."

Even the important crops, the vine, the fig and the olive were destroyed:

Amos 4:9: "I have smitten you with blasting and mildew: when your gardens and your vineyards and your fig trees and your olive trees increased, the palmerworm devoured them: yet have ye not returned unto me, saith the LORD."

(See) Deuteronomy 28:22; Haggai 2:17

Again it says, "Yet have ye not returned unto me, saith the Lord."

Next, the lives of the people were at stake:

Amos 4:10: "I have sent among you the pestilence after the manner of Egypt: your young men have I slain with the sword, and have taken away your horses; and I have made the stink of your camps to come up unto your nostrils: yet have ye not returned unto me, saith the LORD."

(See) Exodus 9:3; Leviticus 26:25; Jeremiah 11:22; 18:21

For the fourth time we read, "Yet have ye not returned unto me, saith the Lord." Then came the overthrow, similar to Sodom and Gomorrah. Doubtless, the sins of those cities were practiced in Samaria during that time.

Amos 4:11: "I have overthrown some of you, as God overthrew Sodom and Gomorrah, and ye were as a firebrand plucked out of the burning: yet have ye not returned unto me, saith the LORD."

(See) Genesis 19:24-25; Deuteronomy 29:23; Isaiah 13:19; Zechariah 3:2

For the fifth time it says, "Yet have ye not returned unto me, saith the Lord."

The End Has Come
Note that this is written in the past tense. Why? Because these destructive judgments are revealed from eternal perspectives. At the time of the proclamation, Israel was doing rather well. But now comes judgment unto destruction. The end is near: "Prepare to meet thy God."

Amos 4:12: "Therefore thus will I do unto thee, O Israel: and because I will do this unto thee, prepare to meet thy God, O Israel."

(See) Isaiah 32:11; Matthew 5:25; 1 Thessalonians 5:2; Revelation 3:3

The worst judgment of all, however, is God turning His back on His people, as we read in verses 4-5. Go ahead, do your religious thing; sacrifice, give tithes and offerings. Nothing will help—the end has come.

> **Amos 4:13:** For, lo, he that formeth the mountains, and createth the wind, and declareth unto man what is his thought, that maketh the morning darkness, and treadeth upon the high places of the earth, The LORD, The God of hosts, is his name."

(See) Job 38:4-7; Psalm 65:6; Isaiah 40:12

The highlight of verse 12 was, "...prepare to meet thy God, O Israel." Now the God of Israel is revealed as the Creator, the Ruler, the ever present God. His words and His doings are final. He controls the universe, and only He can make "the morning darkness."

Our End Times

It seems that we have entered the last stages of the end times. How do we know? Because God does not send judgment in order to warn people and call them back to living faith in Jesus Christ.

I realize that this statement is contrary to the general perception within Churchianity, even among Bible-believing evangelical Christians. Many today insist that the various natural catastrophes are signs of God to call the nations back to repentance. But there is little to no Scriptural evidence that God uses the various natural catastrophes as a prophetic message for the nations today.

That is contrary to the dispensation of grace, under which we now have lived for almost 2,000 years.

Of course, God can punish nations if He so chooses, but to assume that some floods, volcanic eruptions, tornadoes, fires, and earthquakes have a specific purpose in God's plan for the nations cannot be supported in Scripture.

Individual Repentance

One of the reasons is rather simple: God does not call a nation to repentance, but He calls individuals from among the nations, in order to transplant a sinner into His holy nation, the body of Christ, the spiritual temple. A "habitation of God through the Spirit," as Ephesians 2:22 reads.

God permits the very devil, the enemy of our soul, the father of lies, to deceive the bulk of Churchianity, who is no longer interested in the God of Israel, the Creator of heaven and earth, but rather in self-satisfaction.

Prophecy Ignored

It is not surprising, therefore, that interest in the prophetic Word is rapidly declining. Who wants to hear about judgment, catastrophes and Armageddon? After all, we have our own plans; we're waiting for better times. The young people are studying to get better jobs, higher salaries, and the elders are looking forward to retirement, the golden years. Thus, the prophetic Word becomes an unpleasant sideline and is ignored by Churchianity.

Nevertheless, and I am so thankful to write these lines:

175

there are still multitudes of faithful believers, who have their minds and hearts targeted toward the things of God. These are the saints eagerly waiting for the appearing of the Lord: they will not be ashamed at His coming.

Chapter 5

Introduction

While Israel is admonished repeatedly to seek the Lord, the thundering judgment, "I hate, I despise your feast days, and I will not smell in your solemn assembles" (verse 21) is the highlight of this chapter. Israel practiced dual worship. Traditionally, they kept the feasts and holidays, but God exposes their heart, "...the star of your god, which ye made to yourselves" (verse 26).

Prophesied Destruction

Amos 5:1-3: "Hear ye this word which I take up against you, even a lamentation, O house of Israel. 2 The virgin of Israel is fallen; she shall no more rise: she is forsaken upon her land; there is none to raise her up. 3 For thus saith the Lord GOD; The city that went out by a thousand shall leave an hundred, and that which went forth by an hundred shall leave ten, to the house of Israel."

(See) Isaiah 6:13; Jeremiah 7:29; 14:17; Ezekiel 19:1

The horrible destruction of ten-tribe Israel is clearly expressed in the three verses. Again, we must note that this is proclaimed during a time of prosperity, when things are going well; businesses are prospering, crops are plentiful, the government is at ease, and religion has become a comfortable resting pillow.

The "Virgin of Israel"

Who is this *virgin of Israel?* It is the picture of the glory of Israel. The young man desires to have her as wife; she will receive presents and is tenderly cared for. At home, she is protected and receives the best available in the household.

Even today, it is the bride who receives the glory at a wedding. She is the center of attention and admiration; she is destined to be the jewel to her husband. But in this case, all that is now gone; none shall help her, "the virgin of Israel is fallen…forsaken…." Worse yet, the cities will be destroyed, with the population reduced by 90 percent, as evidenced by the words, "an hundred shall leave ten."

While judgment continues to be pronounced upon Israel, a door of grace remains open with this invitation:

Amos 5:4: "For thus saith the LORD unto the house of Israel, Seek ye me, and ye shall live:"

(See) Deuteronomy 4:29; 2 Chronicles 15:2; Isaiah 55:3; Jeremiah 29:13

The statement "Seek ye me, and ye shall live" is addressed to the remnant of the rebellious, ten-tribe house of Israel. There is still grace; there is still time to seek Him.

What Not to Seek

After the invitation, "Seek ye me," the prophet tells Israel what not to seek:

Amos 5:5: "But seek not Bethel, nor enter into Gilgal, and

178

pass not to Beersheba: for Gilgal shall surely go into captivity, and Bethel shall come to nought."

(See) Genesis 21:31-33; 1 Samuel 7:16; 1 Kings 12:28-29

This is just another strong warning for those who have heard the message, "Seek ye me," but refuse to do so.

We read the admonition to seek the Lord in the next verses:

Amos 5:6-9: "Seek the LORD, and ye shall live; lest he break out like fire in the house of Joseph, and devour it, and there be none to quench it in Bethel. 7 Ye who turn judgment to wormwood, and leave off righteousness in the earth, 8 Seek him that maketh the seven stars and Orion, and turneth the shadow of death into the morning, and maketh the day dark with night: that calleth for the waters of the sea, and poureth them out upon the face of the earth: The LORD is his name: 9 That strengtheneth the spoiled against the strong, so that the spoiled shall come against the fortress."

(See) Deuteronomy 4:24; Job 9:9; 12:22; 38:31-34; Isaiah 55:3, 6-7

Israel is being confronted with the absoluteness of the God of Israel, the Creator of heaven and earth; who has power over death and life, and can change the day to night; who controls the movements of the ocean, even the universe.

Joseph, the Blessed One

In verse 6, we notice the name Joseph. He is the blessed one. Here is what his father Jacob-Israel prophesied about him before he died: "Joseph is a fruitful bough, even a fruitful bough by a well; whose branches run over the wall: The archers have sorely grieved him, and shot at him, and hated him: But his bow abode in strength, and the arms of his hands were made strong by the hands of the mighty God of Jacob; (from thence is the shepherd, the stone of Israel:) Even by the God of thy father, who shall help thee; and by the Almighty, who shall bless thee with blessings of heaven above, blessings of the deep that lieth under, blessings of the breasts, and of the womb: The blessings of thy father have prevailed above the blessings of my progenitors unto the utmost bound of the everlasting hills: they shall be on the head of Joseph, and on the crown of the head of him that was separate from his brethren" (Genesis 49:22-26). In blessing Joseph, Jacob reveals Jesus in this prophecy: "the shepherd, the stone of Israel."

Moses on Joseph

It may be helpful to also read the prophecy of Moses regarding Joseph: "And of Joseph he said, Blessed of the LORD be his land, for the precious things of heaven, for the dew, and for the deep that coucheth beneath, And for the precious fruits brought forth by the sun, and for the precious things put forth by the moon, And for the chief things of the ancient mountains, and for the precious things of the lasting hills, And for the precious things of the earth and fulness thereof, and for the good will of him that dwelt in the bush: let the blessing come upon the head of Joseph, and upon the top of the head of him that was separated from his brethren. His glory is like the firstling of his bullock, and his horns are like the horns of unicorns: with them he shall push the people together to the ends of the earth: and they are the ten thousands of Ephraim, and they are the thousands of Manasseh" (Deuteronomy 33:13-17).

We know that Joseph had two sons: Manasseh and Ephraim, born in Africa, half-Egyptian. Because of faithful Joseph, his tribe and sons were blessed abundantly. Particularly Ephraim, who later became the symbol of success and prosperity during the days of the ten-tribe kingdom of Israel.

Israel's Reaction to the Admonition

Amos 5:10-12: "They hate him that rebuketh in the gate, and they abhor him that speaketh uprightly. 11 Forasmuch therefore as your treading is upon the poor, and ye take from him burdens of wheat: ye have built houses of hewn stone, but ye shall not dwell in them; ye have planted pleasant vineyards, but ye shall not drink wine of them. 12 For I know your manifold transgressions and your mighty sins: they afflict the just, they take a bribe, and they turn aside the poor in the gate from their right."

(See) 1 Kings 22:8; Isaiah 1:23; 5:23; 29:21; Micah 6:15; Zephaniah 1:13

Apparently, truth had still been proclaimed at the gate. But the people had become dull of hearing; they outright rejected judgment and righteousness.

One reason for the judgment is particularly emphasized: the mistreatment of the poor.

Today's Poor

It is sobering to realize how often the Lord rebukes those who oppress the poor, yet modern Churchianity brushes it under the carpet with the simple statement, "It's their own fault; they are too lazy to work." Many wealthy believers of the Lord Jesus Christ will one day stand at the Judgment Seat of Christ and will experience the words of James 5:1-6: "Go to now, ye rich men, weep and howl for your miseries that shall come upon you. Your riches are corrupted, and your garments are motheaten. Your gold and silver is cankered; and the rust of them shall be a witness against you, and shall eat your flesh as it were fire. Ye have heaped treasure together for the last days. Behold, the hire of the labourers who have reaped down your fields, which is of you kept back by fraud, crieth: and the cries of them which have reaped are entered into the ears of the Lord of sabaoth. Ye have lived in pleasure on the earth, and been wanton; ye have nourished your hearts, as in a day of slaughter. Ye have condemned and killed the just; and he doth not resist you." In spite of well-developed legal systems, there is no righteous judgment on planet Earth. Righteous judgment is yet to come.

What is the result for Israel?

Amos 5:13: "Therefore the prudent shall keep silence in that time; for it is an evil time."

(See) Ecclesiastes 3:7; Hosea 4:4

In the midst of unrighteousness, when lawlessness becomes law, the words of the prudent, that is the wise, are
silenced. They are no longer heard or accepted because,
"it is an evil time." That means evil is ruling—it is the
hour of darkness.

"Seek Good"

Yet again, we read the Lord's admonition to seek:

Amos 5:14-15: "Seek good, and not evil, that ye may live:
and so the LORD, the God of hosts, shall be with you,
as ye have spoken. 15 Hate the evil, and love the good,
and establish judgment in the gate: it may be that the
LORD God of hosts will be gracious unto the remnant
of Joseph."

(See) Psalm 34:12-16; 97:10; Isaiah 1:16-17; Joel 2:14;
Micah 3:11; 5:3, 7-8; 6:8; Romans 12:9

Another admonition to repent: Seek good...love the
good." This is decision time, either to seek good or evil.
Those who seek good and follow judgment receive the
promise of the grace of God.

Amos 5:16-17: Therefore the LORD, the God of hosts, the
Lord, saith thus; Wailing shall be in all streets; and they
shall say in all the highways, Alas! alas! and they shall

call the husbandman to mourning, and such as are skilful of lamentation to wailing. 17 And in all vineyards shall be wailing: for I will pass through thee, saith the LORD."

(See) Isaiah 16:10; Jeremiah 9:10, 17-20; 48:33

The words "wailing" and "lamentation" stand out, because utter destruction is going to come upon the agricultural prosperity of the land of Israel.

The Day of the Lord

Amos 5:18-20: "Woe unto you that desire the day of the LORD! to what end is it for you? the day of the LORD is darkness, and not light. 19 As if a man did flee from a lion, and a bear met him; or went into the house, and leaned his hand on the wall, and a serpent bit him. 20 Shall not the day of the LORD be darkness, and not light? even very dark, and no brightness in it?"

(See) Isaiah 5:19, 30; Jeremiah 30:7; 48:44; Joel 1:15

Although this is addressed to the ten-tribe Israel in the territory of Samaria, this prophecy reaches into the end times, even to the Great Tribulation. It is the day of the Lord when He reckons with the nations, a day when one will not be able to distinguish between darkness and light. It is all wrapped up in judgment.

The prophet Joel also speaks of this day, "Blow ye the trumpet in Zion, and sound an alarm in my holy mountain: let all the inhabitants of the land tremble: for the day of the LORD cometh, for it is nigh at hand; A day of darkness and of gloominess, a day of clouds and of thick darkness, as the morning spread upon the mountains: a great people and a strong; there hath not been ever the like, neither shall be any more after it, even to the years of many generations" (Joel 2:1-2).

Judgment Seat of Christ

The world will be judged, but so will believers; we must not think that our appearance before the Judgment Seat of Christ will be all glorious. Here is how the Apostle Paul describes that day: "Every man's work shall be made manifest: for the day shall declare it, because it shall be revealed by fire; and the fire shall try every man's work of what sort it is. If any man's work abide which he hath built thereupon, he shall receive a reward. If any man's work shall be burned, he shall suffer loss: but he himself shall be saved; yet so as by fire" (1 Corinthians 3:13-15). This is serious. There are two words I have tried to understand but can't: "suffer loss." Believers who have been saved by His grace, washed in His blood, sealed with the Holy Spirit—yet some "shall suffer loss." This should help us in understanding the phrase, "Woe unto you that desire the day of the Lord!"

Worthless Religion

Amos 5:21-23: "I hate, I despise your feast days, and I will not smell in your solemn assemblies. 22 Though ye offer me burnt offerings and your meat offerings, I will not ac-

185

cept them: neither will I regard the peace offerings of your fat beasts. 23 Take thou away from me the noise of thy songs; for I will not hear the melody of thy viols."

(See) Isaiah 1:11; Micah 6:6-7

This is a strong statement. God actually says: "I hate, I despise...I will not smell...I will not accept...neither will I regard...offerings...I will not hear the melody of thy viols." In other words, "I despise your religious services, if your heart is not dedicated to me and you do not seek after me."

Admonition to Return

Amos 5:24: But let judgment run down as waters, and righteousness as a mighty stream."

How is Israel to do that? They are to seek the Lord. He is the only answer, righteousness and unspeakable grace. That's what we see throughout Scripture; God offers a way of escape, so that we may experience His grace and His peace that passes all understanding.

There is no alternative—it's one or the other; good or evil; light or dark; right or wrong; God or idols!

Amos 5:25-26: "Have ye offered unto me sacrifices and offerings in the wilderness forty years, O house of Israel? 26 But ye have borne the tabernacle of your Moloch and Chiun your images, the star of your god, which ye made to yourselves."

186

(See) Deuteronomy 32:17; Nehemiah 9:18-21; Acts 7:42-43

Israel wanted to have it both ways. They wanted to serve God but also keep their idols, the visible objects they had created for themselves.

Incidentally, that is exactly what the entire world is doing today: worshiping materialism, even at the cost of the poor. This will continue until the very end, as is documented in Revelation 9:20-21: "And the rest of the men which were not killed by these plagues yet repented not of the works of their hands, that they should not worship devils, and idols of gold, and silver, and brass, and stone, and of wood: which neither can see, nor hear, nor walk: Neither repented they of their murders, nor of their sorceries, nor of their fornication, nor of their thefts."

The End of Ten-Tribe Israel
Finally, the prophecy of Israel's dispersion is pronounced in unmistakable terms:

Amos 5:27: "Therefore will I cause you to go into captivity beyond Damascus, saith the LORD, whose name is The God of hosts."

That has been fulfilled; the ten-tribe Israel ceased to exist as an independent national identity before God.

187

Chapter 6

Introduction

While chapter 6 addresses Israel, we notice Zion and David are mentioned, indicating that the people living in luxury and at ease think that their relationship to Judah will be beneficial. Yet in unmistakable terms, God thunders destructive judgments.

Judgment against Zion and Samaria

Amos 6:1: "Woe to them that are at ease in Zion, and trust in the mountain of Samaria, which are named chief of the nations, to whom the house of Israel came!"

(See) Isaiah 32:9-11; Zephaniah 1:12; Luke 6:24

Without ceasing, the prophet exposes the sins of the people of Israel in detail. Verse 1 includes the royal tribe Judah, headquartered in Zion. Apparently, there was a commercial relationship between Israel-Judah and the ten-tribe Israel in Samaria.

Amos 6:2: "Pass ye unto Calneh, and see; and from thence go ye to Hamath the great: then go down to Gath of the Philistines: be they better than these kingdoms? or their border greater than your border?"

(See) Genesis 10:10; 2 Kings 14:25; 2 Chronicles 26:6; Isaiah 10:9

Here is Luther's translation: "Go down to Gath of the Philistines, which were better kingdoms than these, and their borders were further than your borders."

He compares Israel to the neighboring countries, which fought against Israel for generations. In other words, look at those nations and learn from them what happened. They have been reduced to kingdoms of misery. What do you think will happen to you?

Living the Good Life

Amos 6:3: "Ye that put far away the evil day, and cause the seat of violence to come near;"

(See) Ecclesiastes 8:11; Isaiah 47:7; 56:12; Ezekiel 12:27

This indicates that Israel knew there would come a day of judgment, a day of reckoning, but apparently they had such a good time living in luxury, suppressing the poor and taking that which did not belong to them, that they thought, "Judgment is not to come in our time; it's sometime in the future." In other words, prophecy is not going to be fulfilled yet.

Amos 6:4-6: "That lie upon beds of ivory, and stretch themselves upon their couches, and eat the lambs out of the flock, and the calves out of the midst of the stall; 5 That chant to the sound of the viol, and invent to themselves instruments of musick, like David; 6 That drink wine in bowls, and anoint themselves with the chief ointments: but they are not grieved for the affliction of Joseph."

(See) Isaiah 5:12; Ezekiel 34:2-3

Note the words "like David." He was a man after God's own heart. He indeed did great things. Music was one of his loves. Now apostate Israel was imitating David. Obviously, they were deceived in thinking to compare themselves to David, the great musician and lover of the Lord. We see that religion and tradition play a major role, because these people relied on the previous blessings of their nation and the great man of God, King David.

The End of Joseph

One more important item is revealed, namely "the affliction of Joseph." We do know that a special blessing was pronounced upon Joseph. Now, however, nothing was left; Joseph, with Ephraim and Manasseh as part of the ten-tribe rebellious Israel, is being prepared for judgment. Their identity within the ten-tribe Israel is gone forever.

We must qualify this statement. From Scripture, we know that all 12 tribes of Israel will be preserved; they are eternal identities, as documented in Revelation 21:12: "And had a wall great and high, and had twelve gates, and at the gates twelve angels, and names written thereon, which are the names of the twelve tribes of the children of Israel." Thus, the 12 tribes of Israel continue to exist forever, in spite of the fact that ten-tribe Israel ceased to exist.

Ten-Tribe Remnant Added to Judah

Here are a few Scriptures to confirm the integration of

the ten-tribe Israel (remnant): "For the Levites left their suburbs and their possession, and came to Judah and Jerusalem: for Jeroboam and his sons had cast them off from executing the priest's office unto the LORD...And after them out of all the tribes of Israel such as set their hearts to seek the LORD God of Israel came to Jerusalem, to sacrifice unto the LORD God of their fathers...And he gathered all Judah and Benjamin, and the strangers with them out of Ephraim and Manasseh, and out of Simeon: for they fell to him out of Israel in abundance, when they saw that the LORD his God was with him" (2 Chronicles 11:14, 16; 15:9).

Captivity Proclaimed

Amos 6:7-8: "Therefore now shall they go captive with the first that go captive, and the banquet of them that stretched themselves shall be removed. 8 The Lord GOD hath sworn by himself, saith the LORD the God of hosts, I abhor the excellency of Jacob, and hate his palaces: therefore will I deliver up the city with all that is therein."

(See) Leviticus 26:30; Psalm 106:40; Jeremiah 22:5; 51:14

In plain words, the prophet is saying: your living in luxury is coming to an end—you will be first to go into captivity.

Israel Eternal

Why does the Lord God of Israel say: "I abhor the ex-

191

cellency of Jacob"? Here we must recall that the name Jacob means deceiver or supplanter. However, he became a new person, and that new person was called Israel. God actually said: "Thy name shall be called no more Jacob, but Israel" (Genesis 32:28). Yet when we read the next verse, it says: "And Jacob asked him...." Over and again we read the name Jacob. Chapter 35 begins: "And God said unto Jacob...." No mention of Israel; he continues to be called Jacob. Why? Because Israel is prophetic: she will remain for eternity. But Jacob in flesh and blood will not; thus, "I abhore the excellency of Jacob."

Israel was born out of the heart of God. As a matter of fact, the entire universe is subject to the existence of the nation of Israel. This is documented in Jeremiah 31:35-36: "Thus saith the LORD, which giveth the sun for a light by day, and the ordinances of the moon and of the stars for a light by night, which divideth the sea when the waves thereof roar; The LORD of hosts is his name: If those ordinances depart from before me, saith the LORD, then the seed of Israel also shall cease from being a nation before me for ever." When we realize this truth from eternal perspectives, we are comforted regarding to the precarious circumstances Israel finds herself in today. It doesn't matter what the Palestinians do, or what the United States, the United Nations or Europe says or doesn't say; Israel is eternal.

Death to Come

Amos 6:9-11: "And it shall come to pass, if there remain ten

192

men in one house, that they shall die. 10 And a man's uncle shall take him up, and he that burneth him, to bring out the bones out of the house, and shall say unto him that is by the sides of the house, Is there yet any with thee? and he shall say, No. Then shall he say, Hold thy tongue: for we may not make mention of the name of the LORD. 11 For, behold, the LORD commandeth, and he will smite the great house with breaches, and the little house with clefts."

(See) 1 Samuel 31:12; 2 Kings 25:9; Jeremiah 44:26

Let's read verse 9 from the *Tanakh* for a better understanding: "If ten people are left in one house, they shall die." The number 10 represents the law, the Ten Commandments. That means ten men were needed to start a prayer meeting, but that too shall cease because in this case, the ten are dead. Based on my understanding of this Scripture, it means there is no future for the Diaspora Jews; their future lies in the land of Israel.

The answer from the unnamed relative, however, is surprising: "Hold thy tongue: for we may not make mention of the name of the Lord." This is a strict instruction not to mention the name of the Lord. Why not? It is my theory that this points prophetically to the ten-tribe rebellious Israel, which went out of the land, never to return. They lost their identity as an independent nation. In other words, it's the ultimate end for a separate identity from the tribe of Judah.

Another explanation is that when someone dies, the name of the Lord is called upon. In this case, no one should hear the name of the Lord, because the name of the Lord has now become a terror to Israel. One thing is clear: this is the end. When someone can no longer call upon the name of the Lord, then it is utter hopelessness. The prophet goes further to expose the sins of Israel and pronounce judgment:

Amos 6:12-14: "Shall horses run upon the rock? will one plow there with oxen? for ye have turned judgment into gall, and the fruit of righteousness into hemlock: 13 Ye which rejoice in a thing of nought, which say, Have we not taken to us horns by our own strength? 14 But, behold, I will raise up against you a nation, O house of Israel, saith the LORD the God of hosts; and they shall afflict you from the entering in of Hemath unto the river of the wilderness."

(See) 1 Kings 8:65; 2 Kings 14:25; Psalm 75:4-5; Isaiah 28:14-15; 59:13-14; Jeremiah 5:15; Hosea 10:4

Although judgment was coming and apparently was known to the people, they still relied on their own strength. This is evident by their expression: "Have we not taken to us horns by our own strength?" Yet the end did come, and Israel was led into a non-returning captivity, with Samaria destroyed.

What this chapter so vividly shows is that there is no hope, even though they were chosen by God, received the law of God, and had experienced great signs and wonders, the working of the Almighty in their very midst. Why was there no hope? Because their hope was built on their own imagination, which lead them to be brutal oppressors of the poor, disregarding God's law and commandments.

Prosperity Galore

This, incidentally, is a trademark of our prosperous times. We have our religion; our churches are full, and the Christian industry is prospering. But is Jesus, the Son of God, the Messiah of Israel and the Savior of the world, at the center of our activity? That is the question we must ask ourselves in these turbulent times.

Many do not fully realize that a great drought has come upon faithful servants of the Lord, missionary organizations and ministries. They have worked unceasingly in the gospel ministry on mission fields. Many have died there, are buried there, and we will never hear about them. It is sad to say, but many faithful missionaries and ministry workers are paid only to cover their bare existence, yet the Church at large, in most cases, continues to indulge in prosperity.

In closing, let us ask ourselves, have we lived in pleasure on earth and been wanton? Do you hear the cries of the laborers who are reaping the fields? Remember, the Lord of Sabaoth hears them!

Chapter 7

Introduction
The prophet Amos intercedes on behalf of Jacob, and the Lord answers. Amaziah the priest forbids Amos to prophesy, for he is claiming the utter end with the words, "I will not again pass by them any more."

The Five Visions of Amos
Amos 7 begins with the first three of five visions the prophet received, pronouncing the final destruction of ten-tribe Israel.

The First Vision

Amos 7:1-2: "Thus hath the Lord GOD showed unto me; and, behold, he formed grasshoppers in the beginning of the shooting up of the latter growth; and, lo, it was the latter growth after the king's mowings. 2 And it came to pass, that when they had made an end of eating the grass of the land, then I said, O Lord GOD, forgive, I beseech thee: by whom shall Jacob arise? for he is small."

(See) Exodus 10:15; Jeremiah 14:7, 20-21; 42:2; Ezekiel 11:13; Joel 1:4; Nahum 3:15

In this context, the word "grasshopper" should be translated as "locust." These locusts were called to devastate the crops, all but guaranteeing Israel's demise.

Amos' attitude toward the rebellious house of Israel is quite amazing. He prays: "O Lord GOD, forgive, I beseech thee: by whom shall Jacob arise? for he is small." A true prophet always operates with a priestly passion. Immediately, he receives the answer:

Amos 7:3: "The LORD repented for this: It shall not be, saith the LORD."

(See) Deuteronomy 32:36; 1 Chronicles 21:15; Psalm 106:45;
Jeremiah 26:19; Hosea 11:8; Joel 2:14; Jonah 3:10

The Second Vision

Amos 7:4: "Thus hath the Lord GOD showed unto me: and, behold, the Lord GOD called to contend by fire, and it devoured the great deep, and did eat up a part."

(See) Deuteronomy 32:22; Isaiah 66:15-16

Generally, we understand this judgment to result in the withholding of rain, which would mean a great drought. The German Menge translates this verse this way: "I saw how God caused the fire to come up as punishing judgment, devouring the great flood of the ground waters." Water is stronger than fire, yet here we read that the fire devours the water. This reminds us of 1 Kings 18:38: "Then the fire of the LORD fell, and consumed the burnt sacrifice, and the wood, and the stones, and the dust, and licked up the water that was in the trench."
Amos intercedes for Israel again:

Amos 7:5: "Then said I, O Lord GOD, cease, I beseech thee: by whom shall Jacob arise? for he is small."

(See) Psalm 85:4; Joel 2:17

An immediate answer was received:

Amos 7:6: "The LORD repented for this: This also shall not be, saith the Lord GOD."

(See) Psalm 102:17

The Third Vision

Amos 7:7-9: "Thus he showed me: and, behold, the Lord stood upon a wall made by a plumbline, with a plumbline in his hand. 8 And the LORD said unto me, Amos, what seest thou? And I said, A plumbline. Then said the Lord, Behold, I will set a plumbline in the midst of my people Israel: I will not again pass by them any more: 9 And the high places of Isaac shall be desolate, and the sanctuaries of Israel shall be laid waste; and I will rise against the house of Jeroboam with the sword."

(See) Leviticus 26:31; 2 Kings 15:8-10; 21:13; Isaiah 28:17; 34:11;
Lamentations 2:8

A plumb line is a measuring instrument, a tool of judgment that determines right from wrong, straight from crooked, good from evil, light from darkness. The plumb line is used in construction and is the final authority as to whether a pillar, wall or a building is "plumb" or not. The plumb bob that hangs on a string at the bottom of a line cannot lie; it is based on the law of gravity.

Again, we read God's irrevocable statement: "I will not again pass by them anymore." In other words, the independent political identity of the ten rebellious tribes of Israel had no future.

The Priest of Bethel

Amos' proclamation was acknowledged by Amaziah, the priest of Bethel, who reported this to the king:

Amos 7:10-11: "Then Amaziah the priest of Bethel sent to Jeroboam king of Israel, saying, Amos hath conspired against thee in the midst of the house of Israel: the land is not able to bear all his words. 11 For thus Amos saith, Jeroboam shall die by the sword, and Israel shall surely be led away captive out of their own land."

(See) 1 Kings 12:32; 2 Kings 14:23

Amaziah represents the spirit of the false prophet. He makes his message believable: "Amos saith, Jeroboam shall die by the sword." He ignored the fact that it was the Lord who said, "I will rise against the house of Jeroboam with the sword."

Amos was ordered to cease and desist immediately.

Amos 7:12-13: "Also Amaziah said unto Amos, O thou seer, go, flee thee away into the land of Judah, and there eat bread, and prophesy there: 13 But prophesy not again

---

any more at Bethel: for it is the king's chapel, and it is the king's court."

(See) Matthew 8:34; Acts 4:18

Refusal to Heed the Prophetic Word

That is the key to the message for today: refusal to heed the prophetic Word. Without the prophetic Word, we would lose the uniqueness of Holy Scripture. Without the prophetic Word, we would have no light. Without the prophetic Word, we could only aim for a false peace, one that is described in 1 Thessalonians 5:3: "For when they shall say, Peace and safety; then sudden destruction cometh upon them, as travail upon a woman with child; and they shall not escape."

False Prophecy

I must add here that the prophetic Word is not some utterance created by emotions due to circumstances. The prophetic Word is ours; it is Scripture, an essential part of the Gospel message: "We have also a more sure word of prophecy; whereunto ye do well that ye take heed, as unto a light that shineth in a dark place, until the day dawn, and the day star arise in your hearts" (2 Peter 1:19). The prophetic Word separates the Bible from all other books and religions. Prophecy foretells the future. We will not receive the prophetic Word at some later time, but **we have it now.** It is ours and we may read it, search it; in so doing, we are taking heed and receiving light about the future in a place where darkness prevails.

When we allow the prophetic Word to shine into our

200

hearts, then the words we read do not just remain words but become life in our hearts.

Faith and Works

Words of prophecy are useless unless they are accompanied by faith. The religious authority in Jerusalem believed in the written Word. They quoted Scripture, but deep down in their hearts they did not believe. When the pagans from the Far East came to Jerusalem and asked: "Where is He that is born King of the Jews?" we read the reaction of the religious authority: "And they said unto him, In Bethlehem of Judaea: for thus it is written by the prophet, And thou Bethlehem, in the land of Juda, art not the least among the princes of Juda: for out of thee shall come a Governor, that shall rule my people Israel" (Matthew 2:1-6). But apparently, the prophetic Word did not help these priests and scribes. There's no record indicating they went to Bethlehem to pay homage to the newborn King of the Jews.

It was worse in Amos' case, because the prophetic Word was blatantly rejected. It was forbidden to be preached, and the prophet was expelled from the country.

Unauthorized Prophet

Amos makes a peculiar statement in response to Amaziah's commandment:

Amos 7:14-15: "Then answered Amos, and said to Amaziah, I was no prophet, neither was I a prophet's son; but I was an herdman, and a gatherer of sycomore fruit: 15 And

201

the LORD took me as I followed the flock, and the LORD said unto me, Go, prophesy unto my people Israel."

(See) 2 Kings 2:5; Jeremiah 1:7; Ezekiel 2:3-4; Zechariah 13:5

In other words, "I'm not a prophet authorized by the government, nor am I a prophet authorized by a religious organization or a respected seminary. I am a herdsman and a gatherer of sycamore fruit. I just work to make a living. For all practical purposes, I am not authorized to be a prophet at all. Yet the God of Israel said, 'Go, prophesy unto my people Israel.' Who am I to say no? But let it be known that I have received authority from God, and I do pass His message on to the people of Israel." Then he adds:

Amos 7:16-17: "Now therefore hear thou the word of the LORD: Thou sayest, Prophesy not against Israel, and drop not thy word against the house of Isaac. 17 Therefore thus saith the LORD; Thy wife shall be an harlot in the city, and thy sons and thy daughters shall fall by the sword, and thy land shall be divided by line; and thou shalt die in a polluted land: and Israel shall surely go into captivity forth of his land."

(See) 2 Kings 17:6; Isaiah 30:10; Jeremiah 14:16; 29:21, 31-32; Lamentations 5:11; Hosea 4:13-14; Micah 2:6

Once again, we see the ten-tribe Israel without a future. The land was indeed "divided by line." Israel was led into captivity, never to return.

We know today that these prophecies were fulfilled. The ten-tribe Israel no longer exists. However, the remnant of these tribes that did not follow in the footsteps of Jeroboam was integrated into the tribe of Judah, as they came to Jerusalem to worship the God of Israel. They became Jews in order to fulfill the prophecy, "Salvation is of the Jews."

Message to the Gentiles

This holds a clear message for our times: as Gentiles, we stand outside the covenants of Israel, and we must come in humility and repentance to be integrated into the tribe of Judah; that is, the Lion of the Tribe of Judah. He is the Lamb of God who takes away the sins of the world. When we accept the wonderful and glorious truth that our sins have been forgiven, we receive the new birth, which makes us children of God who have a glorious future to look forward to.

We must never forget our hopeless position as Gentiles: "That at that time ye were without Christ, being aliens from the commonwealth of Israel, and strangers from the covenants of promise, having no hope, and without God in the world" (Ephesians 2:12). But praise be to God our Father, for the next verse contains our hope: "But now in Christ Jesus ye who sometimes were far off are made nigh by the blood of Christ."

Jesus, the Living Word of God, guarantees this glorious promise to each and every one of us who believes: "Let not your heart be troubled: ye believe in God, believe also in me. In my Father's house are many mansions: if it were not so, I would have told you. I go to prepare a place for you. And if I go and prepare a place for you, I will come again, and receive you unto myself; that where I am, there ye may be also. And whither I go ye know, and the way ye know" (John 14:1-4).

Chapter 8

Introduction

Declaration of the end of the ten-tribe Israel is reinforced, "The end is come upon my people Israel, I will not again pass by them anymore." The rebellious nation is being utterly cast away, so that a return becomes impossible. This is expressed with the words, "They shall run to and fro to seek the word of the Lord, and shall not find it."

The Fourth Vision

This chapter contains the proclamation of the fourth vision Amos received from God against the people of Israel:

Amos 8:1-2: "Thus hath the Lord GOD showed unto me: and behold a basket of summer fruit. 2 And he said, Amos, what seest thou? And I said, A basket of summer fruit. Then said the LORD unto me, The end is come upon my people of Israel; I will not again pass by them any more."

(See) Jeremiah 1:12; Lamentations 4:18; Ezekiel 7:2-3, 6

This reveals again that there was no hope, no future, and no comfort for the ten-tribe Israel: "The end is come upon my people of Israel."

"Basket of Summer Fruit"

Doubtless, this is the most horrible news Amos hears from God; Israel, God's chosen people, are nothing more than a "basket of summer fruit." We note that the fruit in the basket is separate from the tree, just as the ten-tribe Israel was separated from Judah. The fruit was ripe; in this case, it was ripe for judgment. God pronounced destructive judgment upon His people.

"Cast Forth with Silence"

Amos 8:3: "And the songs of the temple shall be howlings in that day, saith the Lord GOD: there shall be many dead bodies in every place; they shall cast them forth with silence."

The burial of a body is an important event. We note that the kings who served the Lord were lamented over and buried with great honor, while those who did not obey the Lord did not receive such honor.

In this case, the dead were so many that there was no time for proper funerals; the bodies were virtually "cast forth with silence." We already saw this mode of disposing of the body in dishonor in chapter 6, "And a man's uncle shall take him up, and he that burneth him to bring out the bones out of the house" (verse 10). During war, there is no time for mourning the dead or giving proper burial, or to follow the established customs of the land; thus, the bodies are "cast forth with silence."

Revelation of God's Patience

While we have read the prophet's thunderous announce-ment of the coming day of judgment in the previous seven chapters, the Lord saw the need to present addi-tional detail as to what Israel had done against Him and what He will do against Israel as a result of their persist-ent sin. Why did God provide these additional details? I believe it is because of God's long-suffering; He wants to give Israel another chance to repent.

Even in the midst of judgment, God still provides an opportunity to receive grace through repentance.

Inability to Repent

Amos 8:4-6: "Hear this, O ye that swallow up the needy, even to make the poor of the land to fail, 5 Saying, When will the new moon be gone, that we may sell corn? and the sabbath, that we may set forth wheat, making the ephah small, and the shekel great, and falsifying the bal-ances by deceit? 6 That we may buy the poor for silver, and the needy for a pair of shoes; yea, and sell the refuse of the wheat?"

(See) Nehemiah 13:15; Psalm 14:4; Hosea 12:7; Micah 6:10

Here we have another shocking revelation: Israel's inabil-ity and unwillingness to repent. They already heard Amos' words of judgment, but they were oblivious to that coming disastrous day.

We are reminded of God's judgment during the Great Tribulation: "And men were scorched with great heat, and blasphemed the name of God, which hath power over these plagues: and they repented not to give him glory. And the fifth angel poured out his vial upon the seat of the beast; and his kingdom was full of darkness; and they gnawed their tongues for pain, And blasphemed the God of heaven because of their pains and their sores, and repented not of their deeds" (Revelation 16:9-11). They blasphemed God instead of repenting. These people realized that their punishment was coming from God.

Success at Any Cost

In Amos' day, God's words were a hindrance to the people's desire to make a profit through deceitful business practices.

Times have not changed. No one cares that we are actually living in the end stages of the end times. That fact is even ignored by the Church. Doubtless, Amos' messages is very relevant for today.

We may take as an example our modern society. What is the most important thing to make it function? Work, buy, sell, profit. Not long ago, stores were closed throughout the land on Sunday. In some countries, even early Saturday, shops, banks and merchants locked the door and went home for one specific purpose: rest, and in many cases, to contemplate with thanksgiving what God has done. Today, the god of this world is leading man to focus on the stock exchange, investments, profits, possessions. One does not need to be a theological expert to realize that our modern world is sliding toward the absolute worship of possessions.

Great Tribulation Judgment

Amos 8:7-8: "The LORD hath sworn by the excellency of Jacob, Surely I will never forget any of their works. 8 Shall not the land tremble for this, and every one mourn that dwelleth therein? and it shall rise up wholly as a flood; and it shall be cast out and drowned, as by the flood of Egypt."

(See) Psalm 68:34; Hosea 4:3; 8:13

God goes one step further: He reveals to His people the coming judgment of the Great Tribulation:

Amos 8:9: "And it shall come to pass in that day, saith the Lord GOD, that I will cause the sun to go down at noon, and I will darken the earth in the clear day:"

(See) Job 5:14; Isaiah 13:10; Jeremiah 15:9; Micah 3:6;
1 Thessalonians 5:2-3

This is most certainly speaking about the Great Tribulation. Isaiah wrote about it in chapter 13:10: "For the stars of heaven and the constellations thereof shall not give their light: the sun shall be darkened in his going forth, and the moon shall not cause her light to shine." Jeremiah testified: "She that hath borne seven languisheth: she hath given up the ghost; her sun is gone down while it was yet day: she hath been ashamed and confounded: and the residue of them will I deliver to the sword before their enemies, saith the LORD" (Jeremiah 15:9).

Micah proclaimed: "Therefore night shall be unto you, that ye shall not have a vision; and it shall be dark unto you, that ye shall not divine; and the sun shall go down over the prophets, and the day shall be dark over them" (Micah 3:6).

Timeline of Prophecy

This is important to understanding the prophetic Word: we like to have everything presented to us in chronological order, but as is evident from this and other Scriptures, one sentence of a prophetic utterance may bridge thousands of years.

Here an example: the prophet Isaiah speaks of the coming of the Lord and of the great day of tribulation in one breath, "To proclaim the acceptable year of the Lord, and the day of vengeance of our God" (61:2). Approximately 700 years later, Jesus fulfills this prophecy, as we can read in Luke 4:18-19, "The Spirit of the Lord is upon me, because he hath anointed me to preach the gospel to the poor; he hath sent me to heal the brokenhearted, to preach deliverance to the captives, and recovering of sight to the blind, to set at liberty them that are bruised, To preach the acceptable year of the Lord." Note that the Lord stopped reading the Scripture after the words "acceptable year of the Lord," and He closed the book. But the prophet Isaiah continues in one breath, "And the day of vengeance of our God." Why didn't Jesus read that next sentence? Because only a part was fulfilled; thus, in verse 21 of Luke 4 Jesus said, "This day is this scripture fulfilled in your ears."

Famine for God's Word

Amos 8:10: "And I will turn your feasts into mourning, and all your songs into lamentation; and I will bring up sackcloth upon all loins, and baldness upon every head; and I will make it as the mourning of an only son, and the end thereof as a bitter day."

(See) Job 20:23; Isaiah 15:2-3; Jeremiah 6:26; Ezekiel 7:18; Zechariah 12:10

God's Word became hidden because they had deliberately ignored it. That was and is one of the greatest tragedies.

Amos 8:11-12: "Behold, the days come, saith the Lord GOD, that I will send a famine in the land, not a famine of bread, nor a thirst for water, but of hearing the words of the LORD: 12 And they shall wander from sea to sea, and from the north even to the east, they shall run to and fro to seek the word of the LORD, and shall not find it."

(See) 1 Samuel 3:1; 1 Chronicles 15:3; Psalm 74:9; Ezekiel 7:26; Micah 3:6

A time will come when grace has run out, judgment has come, and repentance will not be found. Such was the case with Esau, who sold his birthright for food: "For ye know how that afterward, when he would have inherited the blessing, he was rejected: for he found no place of repentance, though he sought it carefully with tears" (Hebrews 12:17).

211

Too Late

Chapter 8 ends with an irreversible pronunciation of the end of the rebellious ten-tribe Israel as a separate entity:

Amos 8:13-14: "In that day shall the fair virgins and young men faint for thirst. 14 They that swear by the sin of Samaria, and say, Thy god, O Dan, liveth; and, The manner of Beersheba liveth; even they shall fall, and never rise up again."

(See) 1 Kings 12:28-30; Isaiah 41:17; Lamentations 1:18; 2:21; Hosea 2:3; 8:5-6; 10:5; Micah 1:5-6

The idols of Bethel, where they gave an oath, "Thy god, O Dan, liveth," were the curse of Samaria. Even "the fair virgins and the young men" fainted from thirst for the Word of God. They looked in the wrong direction, and thus no help came; it was too late.

Churchianity Oblivious to Its Roots

This prophetic message runs parallel to our time. Churchianity has separated itself from the olive tree, Israel. Romans 11 clearly reveals that the Church has been grafted into the olive tree; we are organically connected to Israel. Note that verse 13 specifically states: "For I speak to you Gentiles." Now read verses 17, 23-24: "And if some of the branches be broken off, and thou, being a wild olive tree, wert graffed in among them, and with them partakest of the root and fatness of the olive tree...And they also, if they abide not still in unbelief, shall be graffed in: for God is able to graff them in again.

212

For if thou wert cut out of the olive tree which is wild by nature, and wert graffed contrary to nature into a good olive tree: how much more shall these, which be the natural branches, be graffed into their own olive tree?" Yes, we are organically connected to Israel. Yet Churchianity is oblivious to its dependence upon Israel. Churchianity has become a "basket of summer fruit," separated from the tree down to its roots.

Ten-Tribe Israel Separated
Such was the case with the ten-tribe Israel. They had separated themselves from Israel proper; that is, from the tribe of Judah.

The Lion of Judah
Let us read again the prophetic blessing of Jacob about Judah: "Judah, thou art he whom thy brethren shall praise: thy hand shall be in the neck of thine enemies; thy father's children shall bow down before thee. Judah is a lion's whelp: from the prey, my son, thou art gone up: he stooped down, he couched as a lion, and as an old lion; who shall rouse him up? The sceptre shall not depart from Judah, nor a lawgiver from between his feet, until Shiloh come; and unto him shall the gathering of the people be" (Genesis 49:8-10).

Therefore, the ten-tribe Israel could not obtain those promises outside the tribe of Judah. It was Judah from which salvation came: "...Behold the Lion of the tribe of Juda, the Root of David, hath prevailed to open the book, and to loose the seven seals thereof" (Revelation 5:5). Later, Jesus said: "Salvation is of the Jews."

213

Israel's national future is anchored in Judah today as well. You must be a Jew to claim Israeli citizenship.

Individual salvation, however, is anchored in the Lion of the Tribe of Judah, Jesus Christ, the Messiah of Israel and Savior of the world. Do you know Him?

Chapter 9

Introduction

Those who had rejected the warnings of the prophet cannot escape God's relentless judgment. He seeks them out wherever they hide. The purpose? "I will destroy it from off the face of the earth." Yet, and this is the wonderful message, that verse continues, "I will not utterly destroy the house of Jacob." The return will only be made possible for the Jews; that is, the fallen tabernacle of David.

The Fifth Vision

Amos 9:1: "I saw the Lord standing upon the altar: and he said, Smite the lintel of the door, that the posts may shake: and cut them in the head, all of them; and I will slay the last of them with the sword: he that fleeth of them shall not flee away, and he that escapeth of them shall not be delivered."

(See) Psalm 68:21; Habakkuk 3:13; Zephaniah 2:14

We can title the first part of chapter 9 "Total Destruction." This is the fifth and last vision Amos passes on in relationship to the sanctuary in Bethel and the irrevocable coming judgment upon Israel. There is no provision for escape for the ten-tribe Israel.

Why, we may ask, is the Lord standing upon the altar? Although some translations say He is standing *beside* the

215

altar, I think standing *upon* it is more precise because it signifies total defeat of the manmade altar. We have to remember that this speaks primarily to the rebellious ten tribes of Israel. It is taking place in Samaria and not in Jerusalem.

Why the destruction of the Temple? Because the Temple represents the manifestation of the invisible God. Recall when the disciples were on the Mount of Olives and said to Jesus, "Behold the temple." It was an object of national pride, an icon the people of Israel could identify with. It was the expression of their hope, aspiration and future.

For Americans, Washington, D.C., the Capitol building, the White House, the flag and the national anthem are objects of national identity, pride and belonging. For the citizen, it becomes a symbol of trust, hope, security and the future—although all temporary.

In Israel's case, judgment is pronounced. That means the people can no longer look to the Temple—their sanctuary, their identity, their hope, their aspiration and their future—because it is now defeated; it is put under the feet of the Lord.

The judgment that came was accomplished through the enemies of Israel. They would destroy the city and the Temple; nothing would be left. Worse yet, the people who would try to flee "shall not be delivered." The survival philosophy that was practiced did not help Israel. While attempting to escape from the enemy, they would still be killed.

Natural Catastrophes

There are different types of escape today. Just think of the various hurricanes and tornados that have plagued the United States in particular. People fled their homes, leaving everything behind, often just to save their lives: not because of enemies, but because of natural catastrophes.

Are Natural Catastrophes Punishment?

Although I have read several articles that seem to indicate that hurricanes are a form of judgment upon the people, I reject this theory. Why? Because we are living in the dispensation of the Church; that is, the dispensation of grace. Natural catastrophes come and go; they were predicted by the Lord Jesus Himself. He said there would be wars and rumors of war, pestilence, famine, earthquakes, etc. Luke actually reports: "Men's hearts failing them for fear, and for looking after those things which are coming on the earth: for the powers of heaven shall be shaken" (Luke 21:26). We know that these types of catastrophes, whether flood, storm, fire, earthquake or volcano, come unexpectedly and at random. They will continue until the Lord comes again. What the Lord did not say is that there should be an increase in wars, pestilence, famines, earthquakes, etc. As a matter of fact, a number of reputable organizations have presented their research indicating that these things are on the decline globally.

Tsunami Judgment?

When the tsunami occurred in Southeast Asia, the flood took many away; Muslims, Hindus, Buddhists, Christians, atheists—there was no difference. Therefore, to pinpoint certain catastrophes and define them as judgment upon a certain group of people, particularly those we don't like or don't agree with, is an error and does not correspond to the spirit of Holy Scripture.

Of course, judgment will come and every nation will be judged in accordance with the righteousness of God. The climax of these judgments will take place at a time defined in Scripture as the Great Tribulation. But for that judgment to take place, the Church of Jesus Christ must be removed. The Church is the salt of the earth and the light of the world, and is the only hindering element for the destructive judgment of God upon the earth.

Israel Is Different

Here in Amos we are dealing with a special people, different from all the people on the face of the earth. No nation can compare themselves to Israel, even the ten-tribe rebellious Israel; it's still one family, one group of people, and that group of people is distinctly different. The prophet Balaam said about Israel, "...the people shall dwell alone, and shall not be reckoned among the nations" (Numbers 23:9).

No Escape

Amos 9:2: "Though they dig into hell, thence shall mine hand take them; though they climb up to heaven, thence will I bring them down:"

(See) Job 20:6; Psalm 139:8; Jeremiah 51:53; Obadiah 4

It doesn't matter whether they try to find safety in the depths of the earth or in the heights; God says He will bring them down. They can't hide in the mountain, nor in the depths of the sea:

Amos 9:3: "And though they hide themselves in the top of Carmel, I will search and take them out thence; and though they be hid from my sight in the bottom of the sea, thence will I command the serpent, and he shall bite them:"

(See) Job 34:22; Jeremiah 16:16; 23:24

One of the only ways of escape was being taken prisoner by the enemy. That would at least secure one's life, with the possibility of being integrated into the enemy nation at some time in the future. But that's not an option here either:

Amos 9:4: "And though they go into captivity before their enemies, thence will I command the sword, and it shall slay them: and I will set mine eyes upon them for evil, and not for good."

(See) Leviticus 17:10; 26:33; Deuteronomy 28:65; Jeremiah 21:10; 39:16

Not only will the enemies of Israel be destructive upon the people, but the Lord God Himself will send judgment:

Amos 9:5: "And the Lord GOD of hosts is he that toucheth

> the land, and it shall melt, and all that dwell therein shall mourn: and it shall rise up wholly like a flood; and shall be drowned, as by the flood of Egypt."

(See) Psalm 104:32; 144:5; Micah 1:4

This does not speak of the enemies, but of "the Lord God of hosts": He is the originator and initiator of judgment.

"The Land Shall Melt"

We note here that God touches the land and the land "melts." As a result, the land rises up like a flood, in comparison with the flood of Egypt. This is God's supernatural judgment upon His people. When He touches the land, something we cannot explain in human terms happens: the geological elements of the land are moved. We know that the waters of Egypt were divided supernaturally. The water rose on each side, and then the water went down from each side, covering Pharaoh and his special forces by a flood. Thus it shall be upon Israel.

The Lord's personal involvement in judging His people is further emphasized in verse 6:

> **Amos 9:6:** "It is he that buildeth his stories in the heaven, and hath founded his troop in the earth; he that calleth for the waters of the sea, and poureth them out upon the face of the earth: The LORD is his name."

(See) Psalm 104:3, 6, 13

The waters of the sea are subject to His command. The

220

Psalmist spoke of Him in Psalm 107:25, 29: "For he commandeth, and raiseth the stormy wind, which lifteth up the waves thereof...He maketh the storm a calm, so that the waves thereof are still." Later in history, Jesus, the Son of God, the Messiah of Israel and the Savior of the world, demonstrated His authority over the sea. We read the testimony in Mark 4:41: "And they feared exceedingly, and said one to another, what manner of man is this, that even the wind and the sea obey him?" Thus we see, God is very personal, involved in the destructive judgment of the ten-tribe Israel nation.

Three Questions

Amos 9:7: "Are ye not as children of the Ethiopians unto me, O children of Israel? saith the LORD. Have not I brought up Israel out of the land of Egypt? and the Philistines from Caphtor, and the Syrians from Kir?"

(See) Deuteronomy 2:23; 2 Kings 16:9; 2 Chronicles 14:9, 12;
Isaiah 20:4; 43:3; Jeremiah 47:4

The great Exodus was the work of God. He brought the children of Israel out of the land of Egypt. Moreover, He also controls the Philistines and the Syrians. Thus, Israel is confronted by the God of creation, who reveals His identity. He is the beginning of Israel; He guides history, but He has now become the judge.

As if all these terrible things, the pronunciation of judgment, were not enough, we continue to read in verse 8:

221

Amos 9:8: "Behold, the eyes of the Lord GOD are upon the sinful kingdom, and I will destroy it from off the face of the earth; saving that I will not utterly destroy the house of Jacob, saith the LORD."

(See) Jeremiah 5:10; 30:11; 44:27

A Little Hope

In the midst of destructive judgment, there is one little glimmer of hope: "...I will not utterly destroy the house of Jacob...." This is the first sign of hope for those who heed the words of the prophet. Yes, Israel was condemned to die; irrevocable judgment was pronounced upon them, and they would be decimated as a nation by the enemies. But they would never be eradicated.

Although verse 9 also pronounces judgment, there too we read of another small glimmer of hope:

Amos 9:9: "For, lo, I will command, and I will sift the house of Israel among all nations, like as corn is sifted in a sieve, yet shall not the least grain fall upon the earth."

(See) Isaiah 30:28; Luke 22:31

Old-time farmers are familiar with this process of sifting the grain, separating the chaff from the wheat. This is the hope for those who, deep down in their heart were waiting for redemption, in spite of the fact they were living in the midst of a sinful, immoral and corrupt nation condemned to die. Not one grain will be destroyed. That is what sifting is all about; the grain is harvested and kept, while the straw and the chaff are rejected.

More Hope

Amos 9:10: "All the sinners of my people shall die by the sword, which say, The evil shall not overtake nor prevent us."

It does not say, "All my people shall die by the sword," but specifically, "All the sinners of my people." Therein lies the difference. Indeed, the ten-tribe Israel ceased to exist, just as prophesied: "…The end is come upon my people of Israel; I will not again pass by them any more" (Amos 8:2b). Again, in chapter 9:8 we read: "I will destroy it from off the face of the earth." Nevertheless, a remnant would be saved. The house of Israel as a separate identity ceased to exist, but the house of Israel integrated into the tribe of Judah, continues to exist until this very day. They are known as Jews.

Judah could not accomplish what God intended for them to accomplish; namely, the salvation of His people and the Gentiles. Yet He who came from Judah, the greatest Jew of all, Jesus Christ, would bring forth salvation. This is recorded for us in Revelation 5:5: "And one of the elders saith unto me, Weep not: behold, the Lion of the tribe of Juda, the Root of David, hath prevailed to open the book, and to loose the seven seals thereof."

The Resurrection of Israel

Amos 9:11: "In that day will I raise up the tabernacle of David that is fallen, and close up the breaches thereof; and I will raise up his ruins, and I will build it as in the days of old:"

(See) Isaiah 16:5; 63:11; Jeremiah 46:26; Acts 15:16

After all the terrible judgments against Israel, including when, "all the sinners of my people shall die," God will do something new.

Before we deal with this fact, we must again emphasize that the entire book of Amos is primarily directed toward the ten-tribe rebellious Israel, but it does not exclude Judah-Israel.

We recall that in chapter 1, God announces judgment upon the neighbor nations, and then He begins with Judah in chapter 2: "Thus saith the LORD; For three transgressions of Judah, and for four, I will not turn away the punishment thereof; because they have despised the law of the LORD, and have not kept his commandments, and their lies caused them to err, after the which their fathers have walked" (verse 4).

While we should make the distinction between Judah-Israel and the ten-tribe rebellious Israel, they are nevertheless one people. Even today, Israel is experiencing tribulation, and worse is yet to come; it is called "Jacob's trouble." Nevertheless, "he shall be saved out of it," says Jeremiah 30:7.

The reason we have determined that the judgments in

224

the book of Amos are primarily directed toward the ten-tribe rebellious Israel, is based on the geography given. We have names such as Samaria, Bethel and Gilgal, places outside the territory of Judah. But, just as in the beginning of the book of Amos, we also see in the end of the same book that all of Israel is included.

The Fallen Tabernacle of David

The "tabernacle of David" definitely refers to Jerusalem; that is, the headquarters of Judah. It is the center of God's dealings with His people. Thus, we are back in the target area of Israel; to be precise, the center of the world.

What does it mean, "the fallen tabernacle of David?" One thing we do know, it does not mean the tent-like tabernacle in which the Ark of the Covenant was housed until David's son Solomon built the Temple. A clue is given: "Close up the breaches thereof; and I will raise up his ruins." This is a description of the physical Temple built of stone in Jerusalem. Ruins indicate masonry buildings; that cannot be said of the tabernacle described for us in Exodus chapters 25—31.

Renewal or Repair?

But then we read the promise: "I will build it as in the days of old." Does that mean that Jerusalem will be re-built exactly as during the days of David? I don't think so. As we study the next few verses, we will recognize that God is planning to do something totally new. Besides, God is not in the repair business.

Unfortunately, Churchianity does the opposite; they

continue eagerly to repair: a better person, better marriage, better family, better children, better health, wealth and happiness. That is the goal of virtually all religions. But God has no intention of repairing anything; rather, He makes all things NEW.

Here it may be helpful to read Jeremiah 31:31: "Behold, the days come, saith the LORD, that I will make a new covenant with the house of Israel, and with the house of Judah." Doubtless, this speaks of the renewal of the people of Israel as God's chosen.

Repairing is man's way; we are always on our way to improving our life, our standard of living, having better products. Even Churchianity seems convinced it can improve man. That is why we have so many false teachings in the church. Even today, the most successful churches and ministries are those which encourage their constituents to "better" their life, under the pretense that by doing so, you will become a better Christian. That, incidentally, is the model of the Freemasons: "Making a better man out of a good one." American Churchianity follows that pattern, by thinking that corrupt man can be repaired in order to create a better society, a greater America.

The New Covenant

God makes a new covenant. What does this new covenant consist of? "But this shall be the covenant that I will make with the house of Israel; After those days, saith the LORD, I will put my law in their inward parts, and write it in their hearts; and will be their God, and they shall be my people. And they shall teach no more every man his neighbour, and every man his brother, say-ing, Know the LORD: for they shall all know me, from the least of them unto the greatest of them, saith the LORD: for I will forgive their iniquity, and I will remem-ber their sin no more" (Jeremiah 31:33-34).

When will that happen? When is the time defined as "after those days"? Here we must turn to the New Tes-tament and read the words James proclaims in Acts 15:14-17: "Simeon hath declared how God at the first did visit the Gentiles, to take out of them a people for his name. And to this agree the words of the prophets; as it is written, After this I will return, and will build again the tabernacle of David, which is fallen down; and I will build again the ruins thereof, and I will set it up: That the residue of men might seek after the Lord, and all the Gentiles, upon whom my name is called, saith the Lord, who doeth all these things."

We note an intermission in God's plan for Israel: "God at the first did visit the Gentiles." Technically speaking, this is not quite correct because He first visited His peo-ple Israel. The first believers were all Jewish people. Later, the Gentiles were added.

What James is saying is that the adding of the Gentiles to the Jewish church will have to be completed first, be-fore God restores Israel spiritually. He must first "take out of them a people for his name."

What will happen afterwards? The fulfillment of Amos 9:11: "In that day will I raise up the tabernacle of David that is fallen, and close up the breaches thereof; and I will raise up his ruins, and I will build it as in the days of old."

Preparation for Resurrection

It stands to reason that this type of fulfillment cannot take place unless preparation is made for the reestablishment of the Jewish people as a sovereign nation in the land of Israel. That, we all know, began on 14 May 1948, when the Jews proclaimed to the world their newly founded state of Israel.

It will be "as in the days of old"; that is, Jerusalem, Israel, God's holy land.

What comes next?

Amos 9:12: "That they may possess the remnant of Edom, and of all the heathen, which are called by my name, saith the LORD that doeth this."

(See) Numbers 24:18; Isaiah 11:14; 43:7; Obadiah 19

This most certainly speaks of the Gentiles, the Church of Jesus Christ, "which are called by my name." Thus, the regathering of Israel is subject to the fullness of the Church from among the Gentiles.

The Great Multitude of Gentiles

James goes one step further in Acts 15. He first speaks of the Gentiles, then of the resurrection and identity of Israel. Finally, in verse 17 he mentions the reason; namely, "That the residue of men might seek after the Lord, and all the Gentiles, upon whom my name is called...." Thus, we may draw a distinction between the Church of Jesus Christ, Israel, and those who will come out of the Great Tribulation after the Church is gone.

228

After Israel is established and judgment comes upon the entire earth, Revelation 7:9 has this to say: "After this I beheld, and, lo, a great multitude, which no man could number, of all nations, and kindreds, and people, and tongues, stood before the throne, and before the Lamb, clothed with white robes, and palms in their hands." This "great multitude" is not the Church; they constitute "the residue of men."

Restoration and Renewal
Next, Amos speaks of the time when God's kingdom is established upon earth:

Amos 9:13: "Behold, the days come, saith the LORD, that the plowman shall overtake the reaper, and the treader of grapes him that soweth seed; and the mountains shall drop sweet wine, and all the hills shall melt."

(See) Genesis 49:11; Leviticus 26:5; Joel 3:18

This is a new thing on earth; it demonstrates uninterrupted harvest and an overabundance of agricultural products. This is not the *old Israel repaired*, but a *new Israel regenerated*. This applies to the people and the land.

Special promises are given to "my people of Israel." Note verse 14:

Amos 9:14: "And I will bring again the captivity of my people of Israel, and they shall build the waste cities, and inhabit them; and they shall plant vineyards, and drink the wine thereof; they shall also make gardens, and eat the fruit of them."

(See) Psalm 53:6; Isaiah 61:4; 65:21; Jeremiah 30:3, 18

Eternity for the Believer

Finally, eternity breaks forth:

Amos 9:15: "And I will plant them upon their land, and they shall no more be pulled up out of their land which I have given them, saith the LORD thy God."

(See) Isaiah 60:21; Ezekiel 34:28; 37:25

God's address to the remnant of the people of Israel does not exclude the land, because the Jews "shall no more be pulled up out of their land."

That, my dear friends, is Israel's true hope. It is the irrevocable "I will" of the God of Israel, who will in the end put all enemies to shame. He will forgive sins and will renew His people, from the least to the greatest; they all will know the Lord.

We have here a wonderful picture of the Church of Jesus Christ. We do not have an earthly promise as does Israel, but a heavenly one; we indeed will harvest without ceasing and have all things in abundance, because we have Him and He has us—the One who gave His life for His Church. He is the One we are eagerly anticipating. That is the goal of the true Christian; it is the answer for our life now and for all eternity.

MICAH

Who Is Like Jehovah?

MICAH

Book of the Bible	God's Directly Spoken Words (%)	Prophecy %*	Significant Names Listed in Each Book						
			Judah	Israel	Ephraim	Jerusalem	Zion	Heathen	Samaria
Hosea	93.32	56	15	44	37	0	0	0	6
Joel	57.70	68	6	3	0	6	7	5	0
Amos	80.95	58	4	30	0	2	2	1	5
Obadiah	97.69	81	1	1	1	2	2	4	1
Jonah	7.39	10	0	0	0	0	0	0	0
Micah	44.88	70	4	12	0	8	9	1	3
Nahum	40.30	74	1	1	0	0	0	0	0
Habakkuk	47.84	41	0	0	0	0	0	2	0
Zephaniah	96.92	89	3	4	0	4	2	1	0
Haggai	67.61	39	4	0	0	0	0	1	0
Zechariah	77.38	69	22	5	3	41	8	5	0
Malachi	93.80	56	3	5	0	2	0	2	0

* Percentage of book as prophecy according to *Tim LaHaye Prophecy Study Bible*

Introduction to Micah

Micah means "Who is like Jehovah?" in English. He receives the Word of the Lord, which exposes the sins of Samaria, as well as Jerusalem. He reveals in particular the sin of oppressing the poor, in a manner similar to Hosea and Amos. Micah prophesies of the fall of the northern kingdom, but also warns about the coming desolation of Judah. His prophetic message is almost evenly divided between Samaria and Jerusalem.

Reading the 16 verses of the first chapter, one cannot but be discouraged. Judgment after judgment, destruction upon destruction, and seemingly unending punishment are destined to come upon the people of Israel.

When we consider the name Micah, "Who is like Jehovah?," then we realize that there is no comparison, there is no likeness in earth or heaven. Jehovah is supreme and, from that position Israel is addressed.

Chapter 1

Introduction

Micah directs his message to Samaria and Jerusalem in the first place, leaving out Israel. But his message includes the whole world, which is evident from the words, "Hearken, O earth, and all that therein is." As the sin and transgression of Jacob in Samaria is uncovered, the saints of Judah are dealt a seemingly harsh measure.

Message to Israel

Micah 1:1: "The word of the LORD that came to Micah the Morasthite in the days of Jotham, Ahaz, and Hezekiah, kings of Judah, which he saw concerning Samaria and Jerusalem."

(See) Jeremiah 26:18; 2 Peter 1:21

Although it is directed toward Samaria and Jerusalem, we must note the important statement in verse 2:

Micah 1:2: "Hear, all ye people; hearken, O earth, and all that therein is: and let the Lord GOD be witness against you, the Lord from his holy temple."

This literally means the entire world.

Armageddon Announcement

Important to notice is that it not only speaks of the imminent judgment that is to befall Judah and Israel, but also goes all the way to the end, the battle of Armageddon:

Micah 1:3-4: "For, behold, the LORD cometh forth out of his place, and will come down, and tread upon the high places of the earth. 4 And the mountains shall be molten under him, and the valleys shall be cleft, as wax before the fire, and as the waters that are poured down a steep place."

(See) Psalm 97:5; Isaiah 26:21; Ezekiel 3:12; Amos 4:13; Nahum 1:5

The prophet Amos spoke in a similar fashion: "For, lo, he that formeth the mountains, and createth the wind, and declareth unto man what is his thought, that maketh the morning darkness, and treadeth upon the high places of the earth, The LORD, The God of hosts, is his name" (Amos 4:13). Isaiah 26:21 says: "For, behold, the LORD cometh out of his place to punish the inhabitants of the earth for their iniquity: the earth also shall disclose her blood, and shall no more cover her slain." This is total judgment upon planet Earth.

Transgression of Jacob

Micah 1:5: "For the transgression of Jacob is all this, and for the sins of the house of Israel. What is the transgression of Jacob? is it not Samaria? and what are the high places of Judah? are they not Jerusalem?"

239

(See) Jeremiah 2:18-19; Hosea 5:5

Samaria is identified as the headquarters of the ten-tribe Israel, while Jerusalem became the center of idolatry for Judah. Jacob is first mentioned, revealing the old nature as his name rightly indicates: "deceiver, supplanter." That very old nature is revealed in Samaria, where idolatry became rampant—worshiping a golden calf. But, Judah is also included because instead of glorifying the name of the Lord in the temple, Judah too became swallowed up in idolatry.

Destruction of Samaria

Micah 1:6-7: "Therefore I will make Samaria as an heap of the field, and as plantings of a vineyard: and I will pour down the stones thereof into the valley, and I will discover the foundations thereof. 7 And all the graven images thereof shall be beaten to pieces, and all the hires thereof shall be burned with the fire, and all the idols thereof will I lay desolate: for she gathered it of the hire of an harlot, and they shall return to the hire of an harlot."

(See) Deuteronomy 9:21; 23:18; 2 Kings 19:25

Today, only a few remnants of ruins are to be found in Samaria, recalling the former glory of the time of the king of Israel.

Not only were the buildings and the idols judged, but also the people:

240

Micah 1:8-9: "Therefore I will wail and howl, I will go stripped and naked: I will make a wailing like the dragons, and mourning as the owls. 9 For her wound is incurable; for it is come unto Judah; he is come unto the gate of my people, even to Jerusalem."

(See) 2 Samuel 1:20; 2 Kings 18:13; Isaiah 13:21-22; Jeremiah 30:12, 15

Here we see the prophet Micah identifying himself with the horrible sins of Judah and Samaria. This is expressed by his testimony, "I will wail...I will go...naked...I will [wail] like the dragons [jackals] ... [mourn] as the owls." With such behavior, he demonstrates the transgressions of his people on the one hand, and his priestly attitude on the other.

No Hope, Even in Jerusalem
The judgment is so terrible that the prophet instructs not to tell Israel's archenemy, the Philistines, who dwell at Gath: "Declare ye it not at Gath."

Micah 1:10-12: "Declare ye it not at Gath, weep ye not at all: in the house of Aphrah roll thyself in the dust. 11 Pass ye away, thou inhabitant of Saphir, having thy shame naked: the inhabitant of Zaanan came not forth in the mourning of Bethezel; he shall receive of you his standing. 12 For the inhabitant of Maroth waited carefully for good: but evil came down from the LORD unto the gate of Jerusalem."

(See) 2 Samuel 1:20; Jeremiah 14:19; Ezekiel 23:29

Saphir means beautiful; Zaanan, rich in herds; Bethezel, a town in Judah; Maroth, bitterness—in spite of being "beautiful" and "rich," still all were disappointing.

Jerusalem was apparently the last hope. But it too becomes hopeless, "evil came down from the Lord." There is simply no good news for Israel. It's all negative. There is no help; the end had come. The enemies are at the gates, and all because Israel violated God's law. They rejected His holy name, and as always is the case, rejection of truth leads to acceptance of a lie.

Mixing Good and Evil

Micah 1:13: "O thou inhabitant of Lachish, bind the chariot to the swift beast: she is the beginning of the sin to the daughter of Zion: for the transgressions of Israel were found in thee."

Lachish was a royal Canaanite city and became a chief fortress of Judah. The mixture is self-evident—Canaanite, Zion, and Israel. Apparently, the difference between Canaan, the pagan, and Judah, God's chosen, had ceased to exist. The prophet identifies it as "the beginning of the sin to the daughter of Zion." Mixture between good and evil cannot but lead to evil. God requires of His people 100 percent faithfulness. He does not accept spiritual "tolerance." It is either one or the other. Here we are reminded of the words addressed to the Church of Laodicea, "I know thy works, that thou art neither cold

242

nor hot: I would thou wert cold or hot. So then because thou art lukewarm, and neither cold nor hot, I will spue thee out of my mouth" (Revelation 3:15-16).

Glory Finds Its End

Micah 1:14: "Therefore shalt thou give presents to Moreshethgath: the houses of Achzib shall be a lie to the kings of Israel."

(See) 2 Kings 16:8

For a clearer understanding, let's read the *Tanakh*: "Truly, you must give a farewell gift to Moreshethgath. The houses of Achzib are to the kings of Israel like a spring that fails." Moreshethgath, the hometown of Micah, will not be saved either.

Micah 1:15: "Yet will I bring an heir unto thee, O inhabitant of Mareshah: he shall come unto Adullam the glory of Israel."

(See) Joshua 15:44; 2 Samuel 23:13

This seems like a veiled hope for the people at Mareshah, because of the name Adullam, which was the cave in which David hid from King Saul. David was a picture of the glory of Israel. Also, the glory of Israel was Jerusalem, but now here at Achzib, the glory finds its end:

243

Micah 1:16: "Make thee bald, and poll thee for thy delicate children; enlarge thy baldness as the eagle; for they are gone into captivity from thee."

(See) 2 Kings 17:6; Isaiah 22:12

There is no encouragement whatsoever. God's judgment upon His people is complete: "For her wound is incurable."

Summary

While these judgments did take place, we have to remember what we read at the beginning; namely, that the judgment of the world is included. In a package which God presents through His prophets, judgment will be finalized at the battle of Armageddon, the place where all the nations of the world will ultimately be judged righteously.

When we read these verses, we realize the seriousness of violating God's law. It is irreparable. There is no way back, no escape and no way out.

Yet there is one Way, the one Person who stated: "I am the way." He is Israel's hope, and He is the hope of all who confess that their lives have not matched up to the requirements of God. Judgment had to be executed upon the nation of Israel, both the ten-tribe Israel and the house of Judah. And judgment must also be executed upon each person on planet Earth. Blessed is he who believes in the substitute; namely, that judgment has been executed upon the perfect One, the sinless One, Jesus Christ of Nazareth. He took the punishment of sin upon Himself when He was nailed to the cross. Believing in that fact is the only way to escape the ultimate judgment.

Chapter 2

Introduction

God's patience, long-suffering and compassion become evident when reading the prophets. But that does not mean in any way that God overlooks Israel's sins. One would think it is sufficient just to tell Israel that they have sinned, and as a result, they will be punished by the enemies and the remnant deported to foreign countries, to serve foreigners. That would be a short summary. But such is not the case. The prophet lists, item-by-item, all the things Israel has perpetrated against each other and against the commandment of God.

This leads me to the conclusion that when we as believers stand before the judgment seat of Christ, there will not be a blanket pardon. Rather, Luke 12:2 will be fulfilled: "For there is nothing covered, that shall not be revealed; neither hid, that shall not be known." Whatever we try to hide now will be exposed openly.

The assumption seems popular that once you are saved, everything is glory. Of course, we are saved once and for all for eternity—that is assured in Holy Scripture. Nevertheless, after we have become believers and our time on earth is over, there will be a reckoning of every moment of our life: each word, deed, even our very thoughts will be exposed.

It could be extremely uncomfortable if the deepest thoughts of our heart were exposed; it would be embarrassing to no end. For that reason, we are repeatedly admonished to effect a change of mind. Our direction, our goal, our motive and desire must be changed. This can only be done through total dedication to the One who walked before us, who sacrificed Himself for our sakes. It was the Apostle Paul who could say, "I am crucified with Christ: nevertheless I live; yet not I, but Christ liveth in me: and the life which I now live in the flesh I live by the faith of the Son of God, who loved me, and gave himself for me" (Galatians 2:20). This must become a reality in each of our lives.

Total Exposure of Sin

Micah 2:1: "Woe to them that devise iniquity, and work evil upon their beds! when the morning is light, they practise it, because it is in the power of their hand."

(See) Esther 3:8-9; Psalm 7:11-14; 36:4; Isaiah 32:7; Hosea 7:6; Nahum 1:11

At the time of this prophecy, most Israelis were doing rather well. Accumulation of possessions and riches was the fashion of the day. They were thinking of gain even while asleep. They were planning how to obtain fields and houses by deceit, taking someone else's inheritance.

Micah 2:2: "And they covet fields, and take them by violence; and houses, and take them away: so they oppress a man and his house, even a man and his heritage."

(See) 1 Kings 21:1-15; Isaiah 5:8; Jeremiah 22:17; Amos 8:4

False Blessing in the Church

There is a strange spirit going around these days; it praises success and material accumulation, and calls it blessing. Yet when reading Holy Scripture, we see that such should not be the aim or motive of our lives. There is not one instance in the Bible where the poor is condemned and the rich is praised. Actually, the word "rich" appear 40 times in the New Testament, and is virtually always negatively portrayed, while the word "poor" is listed 35 times, and each time in a comforting light.

We already saw in Luke 12:2 that everything will be revealed. Jesus specifically emphasizes the difference between the spiritual life and the life in the flesh: "Take heed, and beware of covetousness: for a man's life consisteth not in the abundance of the things which he possesseth" (Luke 12:15).

Israel's Sin Uncovered

Micah 2:3: "Therefore thus saith the LORD; Behold, against this family do I devise an evil, from which ye shall not remove your necks; neither shall ye go haughtily: for this time is evil."

(See) Deuteronomy 28:48; Isaiah 2:11-12; Jeremiah 8:3; 18:11; Lamentations 1:14; 5:5; Amos 3:1-2; 5:13

There is no escape; God will execute righteous judgment upon evil. For Israel, it will be so bad that even foreigners will take notice:

247

Micah 2:4-5: "In that day shall one take up a parable against you, and lament with a doleful lamentation, and say, We be utterly spoiled: he hath changed the portion of my people: how hath he removed it from me! turning away he hath divided our fields. 5 Therefore thou shalt have none that shall cast a cord by lot in the congregation of the LORD."

(See) Deuteronomy 32:8-9; Joshua 18:10; Jeremiah 9:10, 17-21; Habakkuk 2:6

God's law had ceased to be implemented in the land of Israel; that was the great tragedy. Now it is God who changes the blessing into a curse.

Opposition to Prophecy

Micah 2:6: "Prophesy ye not, say they to them that prophesy: they shall not prophesy to them, that they shall not take shame."

(See) Isaiah 30:10; Amos 2:12; 7:16

The *Tenakh* reads: "Do not prophesy about these things: disgrace will not overtake us." In other words, Israel was saying, "We will not hear prophecy regarding shame and disgrace, because we are doing well."

Micah 2:7: "O thou that art named the house of Jacob, is the spirit of the LORD straitened? are these his doings? do not my words do good to him that walketh uprightly?"

(See) Psalm 84:11; 119:68; Isaiah 59:1

Note the words "house of Jacob"; that means the literal, physical, flesh-and-blood people of Israel.

There is no heeding of the Word of God, no understanding of His judgment, and no believing in the work of the Holy Spirit.

Lawlessness Tolerated

Micah 2:8-9: "Even of late my people is risen up as an enemy: ye pull off the robe with the garment from them that pass by securely as men averse from war. 9 The women of my people have ye cast out from their pleasant houses; from their children have ye taken away my glory for ever."

(See) Psalm 120:6-7; Jeremiah 12:8; Ezekiel 39:21

Lawlessness, theft and brutality are committed without remorse. Unrighteousness is in the hands of those who have power.

Micah 2:10: "Arise ye, and depart; for this is not your rest: because it is polluted, it shall destroy you, even with a sore destruction."

(See) Deuteronomy 12:9; Psalm 106:3-8

Those who think differently are encouraged to escape from the coming destruction.

Micah 2:11: "If a man walking in the spirit and falsehood do lie, saying, I will prophesy unto thee of wine and of strong drink; he shall even be the prophet of this people."

(See) Isaiah 28:7; Jeremiah 5:31

This is an exposure of the desire of the people; they would rather believe a lie than heed the prophet's proclamation of truth. Wine and strong drink lead to illusion, away from reality; in this case, away from God's truth.

"Don't Be Negative"

Such is also the case today. By no means say or write anything that can be interpreted as offensive, negative or divisive. The spirit of the end times says, "Preach only the good and positive; give people hope here on earth, and the Lord will bless you abundantly." But, quite apparently, that's not God's message. He has not given us prophets who paint a rosy picture of the future. What does Jesus say about the future? "For then shall be great tribulation, such as was not since the beginning of the world to this time, no, nor ever shall be" (Matthew 24:21). That's not positive at all.

A Little Hope

Nevertheless, there is a glimmer of hope for the remnant of Israel:

Micah 2:12: "I will surely assemble, O Jacob, all of thee; I will surely gather the remnant of Israel; I will put them together as the sheep of Bozrah, as the flock in the midst of their fold: they shall make great noise by reason of the multitude of men."

(See) Isaiah 11:11; Micah 4:6-7; Zephaniah 3:19

Note again that He uses both names, *Jacob* and *Israel*. Jacob identifies the nature of sin. The name means "deceiver" or "supplanter," while Israel could be translated in English with the words "God's warrior," or "having power with God." This shows that God will do a work in the last days that will be astonishing. He will bring Jacob back to the land of Israel, and there Jacob will become a "multitude of men."

Micah 2:13: "The breaker is come up before them: they have broken up, and have passed through the gate, and are gone out by it: and their king shall pass before them, and the LORD on the head of them."

This verse means that under their own power, Jacob, under the banner of Zionism, will break out of the straitjacket of the Diaspora, return to the land of the fathers, and in the end will experience salvation. "The Lord on the head of them" will be a reality.

Chapter 3

Introduction

With precision, the prophet Micah exposes the leaders of the people, the lies of the prophets, and the brutality of the evil shepherds.

Judgment upon the House of Israel

Micah 3:1: "And I said, Hear, I pray you, O heads of Jacob, and ye princes of the house of Israel; Is it not for you to know judgment?"

(See) Psalm 82:1-5; Jeremiah 5:4-5

The leaders of Israel were expected to know the law, to know judgment; that was a given. But they neglected to practice it. Therefore, the sins of the leaders and the princes of Israel are mercilessly exposed.

Micah 3:2-3: "Who hate the good, and love the evil; who pluck off their skin from off them, and their flesh from off their bones; 3 Who also eat the flesh of my people, and flay their skin from off them; and they break their bones, and chop them in pieces, as for the pot, and as flesh within the caldron."

(See) Psalm 14:4; 53:4; Ezekiel 11:6-7; 22:27; Zephaniah 3:3

This is extremely shocking; it shows that the leadership, the rich and the powerful, were oppressing the people excessively. Psalm 14:4 refers to it: "Have all the workers of iniquity no knowledge? who eat up my people as they eat bread, and call not upon the LORD." This does not refer to literally eating the people, but subjecting them to such brutality that they were totally used up—all for the pleasure and the benefit of the ones in power.

The Lord Shall Not Answer

Micah 3:4: "Then shall they cry unto the LORD, but he will not hear them: he will even hide his face from them at that time, as they have behaved themselves ill in their doings."

(See) Deuteronomy 31:17; Proverbs 1:28; Isaiah 1:15; 59:2; Jeremiah 11:11

Here we see the ultimate punishment: separation from God. God will not hear; He will hide Himself from His people. Without God, there is darkness, no hope, no future. With God, there is light, there is forgiveness, there is salvation, but the latter will not be available to them "at that time." That is the time of the Gentiles, beginning with Nebuchadnezzar of Babylon and ending with "Mystery Babylon." During "that time" Israel would not have the opportunity to be a free and independent nation.

Prophets for Profit

Micah 3:5: "Thus saith the LORD concerning the prophets that make my people err, that bite with their teeth, and cry, Peace; and he that putteth not into their mouths, they even prepare war against him."

(See) Isaiah 9:15-16; Jeremiah 6:14; 14:14-15

The *Tanakh* reads: "Thus saith the LORD to the prophets who lead My people astray, who cry 'Peace!' when they have something to chew, but launch a war on him who fails to fill their mouths." They prophesied the "good news" for the people who paid well, yet refused anyone unable or unwilling to pay. Worse yet, these prophets went so far as to "prepare war against him."

Micah 3:6-7: "Therefore night shall be unto you, that ye shall not have a vision; and it shall be dark unto you, that ye shall not divine; and the sun shall go down over the prophets, and the day shall be dark over them. 7 Then shall the seers be ashamed, and the diviners confounded: yea, they shall all cover their lips; for there is no answer of God."

(See) Psalm 74:9; Isaiah 59:10; Ezekiel 13:23; Amos 8:11

Here we see darkness coming over the prophets, "there is no answer of God." We realize that they, the seers and the diviners, believed in the God of Israel; they proclaimed His message with apparent total conviction, but their unrighteous deeds separated them from the living God. Not following truth will always lead to embracing lies.

Micah Is Different

Micah, whose name means, "Who is like Jehovah?" strictly separates himself from the prophecy-for-money prophets with the following testimony:

Micah 3:8: "But truly I am full of power by the spirit of the LORD, and of judgment, and of might, to declare unto Jacob his transgression, and to Israel his sin."

(See) Isaiah 58:1; 61:1-2; 1 Corinthians 2:1, 4

There was no second guessing with the prophet Micah. He distinguished himself from the others prophets, "full of power by the spirit of the LORD, and of judgment."

This is an extremely important sentence; it reveals that we can proclaim the truth of the Gospel effectively only in the power of the Spirit of God. How can one obtain this power of the Spirit? By being empty of self. Only an empty vessel can be filled with the Holy Spirit.

No Messianic Preparation

Micah 3:9: "Hear this, I pray you, ye heads of the house of Jacob, and princes of the house of Israel, that abhor judgment, and pervert all equity."

(See) Psalm 58:1-2; Isaiah 1:23

255

This behavior is diametrically opposed to God's instruction in preparation for the coming of the Messiah. Instead of making the path straight, they "abhor judgment, and pervert all equity."

We recall what John the Baptist told the Pharisees in John 1:23: "...I am the voice of one crying in the wilderness, Make straight the way of the Lord, as said the prophet Esaias." "Make straight the way" means to proclaim truth and justice, to practice and uphold it.

Corrupt Trio: Judge, Priest and Prophet

Moreover, the terrible brutality of deliberate rebellion against God is revealed:

Micah 3:10-11: "They build up Zion with blood, and Jerusalem with iniquity. 11 The heads thereof judge for reward, and the priests thereof teach for hire, and the prophets thereof divine for money: yet will they lean upon the LORD, and say, Is not the LORD among us? none evil can come upon us."

(See) 1 Samuel 4:5-6; Isaiah 1:23; 48:2; Jeremiah 6:13; Ezekiel 22:12; Titus 1:11

Here the proclaimers of the Word of God are specifically targeted: the priests and the prophets. The priest's task was to present the people to God, and the prophet's calling was to proclaim the message of God to the people. Quite obviously, they had made it a business; it was a matter of making money, success by all means—the more the better.

Note, however, that they do it in the name of the Lord. They proclaim a partial truth, namely that the *Lord* is in their midst; subsequently, peace, security and prosperity will continue indefinitely. That corresponds to today's popular teaching: religion equals prosperity and peace.

The Church Today

We don't need to be accomplished theologians to understand that this message is just as applicable to the Church today as it was long ago to Israel. When we look at our churches in general, we find great prosperity: never have we been so rich, so prosperous, and so filled with many good things as today. Yet, the most important thing is neglected; namely, the spiritual state of the Church; the deliberate refusal to heed the prophetic Word.

It has become unpopular to expose teachings that are contrary to Scripture. But, didn't Jesus clearly prophesy that such would come? "For there shall arise false Christs, and false prophets, and shall show great signs and wonders; insomuch that, if it were possible, they shall deceive the very elect" (Matthew 24:24). Those who heed the prophetic Word will not hope for better times, more righteousness, or the election of a so-called Christian government. Believers who read the prophetic Word know what is to come in the near future. So, what are we to do? "Therefore be ye also ready: for in such an hour as ye think not the Son of man cometh" (Matthew 24:44).

Total Destruction

Hope for the future was taken away from Jacob and Israel. Even more, from their beloved Zion and Jerusalem, including the glorious house of the Lord. All was placed under the coming judgment:

Micah 3:12: "Therefore shall Zion for your sake be plowed as a field, and Jerusalem shall become heaps, and the mountain of the house as the high places of the forest."

(See) Psalm 79:1; Jeremiah 9:11; 26:18

Micah thunders a message no one wanted to hear: the total destruction of the city of Jerusalem and their beloved temple. About 150 years later, the book of Jeremiah confirms the devastating proclamation of judgment, "Micah the Morasthite prophesied in the days of Hezekiah king of Judah, and spake to all the people of Judah, saying, Thus saith the LORD of hosts; Zion shall be plowed like a field, and Jerusalem shall become heaps, and the mountain of the house as the high places of a forest. Did Hezekiah king of Judah and all Judah put him at all to death? did he not fear the LORD, and besought the LORD, and the LORD repented him of the evil which he had pronounced against them? Thus might we procure great evil against our souls" (26:18-19).

Chapter 4

Introduction

This chapter shows the other side of the horrific judgment that comes upon Jerusalem. It's a message of hope, the message of the coming of the Messiah. We may title it, "Through Judgment toward Salvation."

The Last Days

Chapter 4 begins with the word "but," which denotes a change of condition:

Micah 4:1: "But in the last days it shall come to pass, that the mountain of the house of the LORD shall be established in the top of the mountains, and it shall be exalted above the hills; and people shall flow unto it."

(See) Isaiah 2:2; Daniel 2:44; Zechariah 8:3

We would immediately want to know, when are these "last days"? The prophet Joel describes a particular event that would initiate the last days. It is recorded in Acts 2:16-18: "But this is that which was spoken by the prophet Joel; And it shall come to pass in the last days, saith God, I will pour out of my Spirit upon all flesh: and your sons and your daughters shall prophesy, and your young men shall see visions, and your old men shall dream dreams: And on my servants and on my handmaidens I will pour out in those days of my Spirit; and

259

they shall prophesy."

When we read the book of Acts and the epistles, we quickly realize that these signs were fulfilled. However, Peter does not just quote these three verses; he continues: "And I will show wonders in heaven above, and signs in the earth beneath; blood, and fire, and vapour of smoke: The sun shall be turned into darkness, and the moon into blood, before that great and notable day of the Lord come" (verses 19-20). These supernatural signs will take place at the end of the last days; or, to be more precise, during the Great Tribulation. Thus, "the last days" means the dispensation of the Church on earth.

Jerusalem Exalted

The Lord's absolute authority will be established in Jerusalem; the mountains "shall be exalted." That doesn't mean the mountain will grow larger or higher, but it is a picture of absolute geographic, physical and spiritual power. A mountain is often used in Scripture to manifest power. Castles for example, were built on mountaintops because of the advantage of height when facing the enemy.

Another important point is what Daniel the prophet reveals about Nebuchadnezzar's dream: "Thou sawest till that a stone was cut out without hands, which smote the image upon his feet that were of iron and clay, and brake them to pieces. Then was the iron, the clay, the brass, the silver, and the gold, broken to pieces together, and became like the chaff of the summer threshingfloors; and the wind carried them away, that no place was found for them: and the stone that smote the image became a

great mountain, and filled the whole earth" (Daniel 2:34-
35). Naturally, this passage is referring to the Lord Jesus
Christ. He is not a literal mountain, but He is the absolute power—not only in Jerusalem or Israel, but also
over "the whole earth."

Jerusalem: World Headquarters

Micah 4:2: "And many nations shall come, and say, Come,
and let us go up to the mountain of the LORD, and to
the house of the God of Jacob; and he will teach us of
his ways, and we will walk in his paths: for the law shall
go forth of Zion, and the word of the LORD from
Jerusalem."

(See) Isaiah 2:3; Zechariah 2:11; 14:16; John 6:45

Apparently, the judicial institutions of the world's nations will no longer be decisive. In the U.S., for example,
the Constitution and all its amendments will be nullified:
"the law shall go forth of Zion"!

It seems significant that it says, "the house of the God
of Jacob" and not, "the house of the God of Israel." This
is because sin will still be present but will be judged righteously during the 1,000-year Kingdom of Peace. In other
words, people living during the 1,000-year Kingdom of
Peace will not automatically experience the rebirth; they
will not be new creatures in Christ, but they will be sinners under the law of Christ. Sin will be judged during
the Lord's reign. Only saints will survive during the
1,000-year Kingdom of Peace.

261

Ultimate Gun Control

The nations will be disarmed; military training camps, schools and academies will be closed. There will be no more weapons and no more war.

Micah 4:3: "And he shall judge among many people, and rebuke strong nations afar off; and they shall beat their swords into plowshares, and their spears into pruninghooks: nation shall not lift up a sword against nation, neither shall they learn war anymore."

(See) Psalm 72:7; Isaiah 2:4; Hosea 2:18; Joel 3:10; Luke 1:33

Today, however, Matthew 24:6 applies: "Ye shall hear of wars and rumors of wars." But when Jesus comes, all wars will end. How? By the prohibition of all weapons. That will be the ultimate "gun control law."

Fight for Freedom?

It doesn't matter what history book you read, or what country you are concerned with: every nation on earth honors its soldiers and proudly proclaims that these brave men and women laid down their lives so that we may enjoy freedom. If, however, that were true, we would have had peace a long time ago. The problem lies in the question: who are the enemies? We conveniently overlook the fact that peace and freedom mean different things to different people. Therefore, the term "freedom fighters" stands in contrast to our Lord's statement regarding freedom. Only after the weapons have been abolished shall they not "learn war any more." Then, for the first time, we will have true freedom, but not before.

Real peace and freedom is offered even now through faith in Christ. Jesus said, "Peace I leave with you, my peace I give unto you, not as the world giveth, give I unto you" (John 14:27).

Peace for Israel
While the first three verses include all the nations of the world, the next two are specifically directed toward Israel:

Micah 4:4-5: "But they shall sit every man under his vine and under his fig tree; and none shall make them afraid: for the mouth of the LORD of hosts hath spoken it. 5 For all people will walk every one in the name of his god, and we will walk in the name of the LORD our God for ever and ever."

(See) Exodus 3:14-15; 1 Kings 4:25; Isaiah 1:20; 40:5; Jeremiah 30:10; Zechariah 3:10

This is future: Israel will experience true peace. While the nations will follow the name of their gods, in the end it will lead to the recognition of Jehovah, the God of Israel.

Return of the Jews to Israel

Micah 4:6-7: "In that day, saith the LORD, will I assemble her that halteth, and I will gather her that is driven out, and her that I have afflicted; 7 And I will make her that halted a remnant, and her that was cast far off a strong nation: and the LORD shall reign over them in mount Zion from henceforth, even for ever."

(See) Psalm 147:2; Isaiah 56:8; Jeremiah 3:18; Ezekiel 34:13, 16; Daniel 7:14; Zephaniah 3:19; Luke 1:33; Revelation 11:15

Today, we are witnessing a partial fulfillment: the Jews are returning to their land. Yet, the Lord does not reign from Mount Zion. While the gathering has begun, it is not the end; it will continue until all Jews of the world have returned to Israel. This is confirmed by the prophet Ezekiel, "Then shall they know that I am the LORD their God, which caused them to be led into captivity among the heathen: but I have gathered them unto their own land, and have left none of them any more there" (Ezekiel 39:28).

The return of the Jews to the land of Israel today is not the final fulfillment of prophecy. It is part of the progressive fulfillment in preparation for the final fulfillment.

The Lord Comes to Zion

Micah 4:8: "And thou, O tower of the flock, the strong hold of the daughter of Zion, unto thee shall it come, even the first dominion; the kingdom shall come to the daughter of Jerusalem."

(See) Psalm 48:3, 12; 61:3

264

This is significant, because the *daughter of Zion* is a description of the Jewish people. They will not *come to the Lord,* but the opposite is true; *the Lord shall come to them.*

This is God's initiative of grace, also confirmed by the prophet Zechariah: "And I will pour upon the house of David, and upon the inhabitants of Jerusalem, the spirit of grace and of supplications: and they shall look upon me whom they have pierced, and they shall mourn for him, as one mourneth for his only son, and shall be in bitterness for him, as one that is in bitterness for his firstborn" (Zechariah 12:10).

Return from Babylon

Micah 4:9-10: "Now why dost thou cry out aloud? is there no king in thee? is thy counsellor perished? for pangs have taken thee as a woman in travail. 10 Be in pain, and labour to bring forth, O daughter of Zion, like a woman in travail: for now shalt thou go forth out of the city, and thou shalt dwell in the field, and thou shalt go even to Babylon; there shalt thou be delivered; there the LORD shall redeem thee from the hand of thine enemies."

(See) Isaiah 43:14; 45:13; 48:20; Jeremiah 8:19

It was not the time during those days for Israel to experience the birth of the King. According to the study notes in the margin of my Bible, another 750 years had to pass before Jesus was born.

But why does the prophet tell the people that they shall

be delivered in Babylon? What happened during the Babylonian captivity? Did Israel experience salvation? Not at all; they remained there in captivity. Yet something important happened. This is how the book of Ezra begins, "Now in the first year of Cyrus king of Persia, that the word of the LORD by the mouth of Jeremiah might be fulfilled, the LORD stirred up the spirit of Cyrus king of Persia, that he made a proclamation throughout all his kingdom, and put it also in writing, saying, Thus saith Cyrus king of Persia, The LORD God of heaven hath given me all the kingdoms of the earth; and he hath charged me to build him an house at Jerusalem, which is in Judah. Who is there among you of all his people? his God be with him, and let him go up to Jerusalem, which is in Judah, and build the house of the LORD God of Israel, (he is the God,) which is in Jerusalem" (Ezra 1:1-3).

The Birth of Jewish Identity

Who was to return to Jerusalem and build the Temple? The tribe of Judah. That means the Jews were established as an *identity* in Babylon. This is the birth of the Jewish identity.

We have to understand that besides the tribe of Judah, other tribes were also in Babylon, as evident from Ezra 1:5, "Then rose up the chief of the fathers of Judah and Benjamin, and the priests, and the Levites...." They all were integrated into the tribe of Judah, hence became Jews.

This ingathering of the remnant of the tribes of Israel is also recorded in 2 Chronicles 11:16, "And after them out of all the tribes of Israel such as set their hearts to seek the LORD God of Israel came to Jerusalem, to sacrifice unto the LORD God of their fathers." Later in 2 Chronicles 15:9 we read, "And he gathered all Judah and Benjamin, and the strangers with them out of Ephraim and Manasseh, and out of Simeon: for they fell to him out of Israel in abundance, when they saw that the LORD his God was with him." The children of the tribes of Israel do not constitute the ten lost tribes, but remnants were integrated into the tribe of Judah, "Be in pain, and labor to bring forth, O daughter of Zion, like a woman in travail." That is the birth of the Jewish identity.

Zion Resurrected

Micah 4:11-13: "Now also many nations are gathered against thee, that say, Let her be defiled, and let our eye look upon Zion. 12 But they know not the thoughts of the LORD, neither understand they his counsel: for he shall gather them as the sheaves into the floor. 13 Arise and thresh, O daughter of Zion: for I will make thine horn iron, and I will make thy hoofs brass: and thou shalt beat in pieces many people: and I will consecrate their gain unto the LORD, and their substance unto the Lord of the whole earth."

(See) Isaiah 5:25-30; 60:9; Jeremiah 51:20-23; Revelation 21:24

We know from history that Jerusalem has been destroyed about 14 times by various Gentile powers. Indeed, Zion was defiled on multiple occasions. But Zion is the key word for Israel's resurrection as a nation. Zionism simply means the return of the Jews to Zion, and that return in itself is the preparation for the judgment of the nations.

The nations surrounding Israel have experienced how Zion "beat in pieces many people." Lebanon, Syria, Jordan, and Egypt have been beaten severely several times. But countries not bordering Israel, such as Iraq, Iran, and in recent time, Sudan and Uganda have also experienced Zion's power.

But the rest of the world is not exempt: they too will be judged by "the daughter of Zion, "Arise and thresh, O daughter of Zion: for I will make thine horn iron, and I will make thy hoofs brass: and thou shalt beat in pieces many people." Salvation is of the Jews, but so is judgment.

All Nations Oppose Zion

It is not surprising that not one nation in the world agrees with Holy Scripture, which identifies Zion—Jerusalem—as God's residence on earth. Thus, the nations take it upon themselves to defile Zion by dividing up the land between the Jews and the Arab nations, with Churchianity having a significant say about the future of this city.

Someone may ask, "What is Churchianity?" Answer: it is the last Gentile superpower, consisting of the European nations and the countries they established in colonial times. These European nations had one thing in common: the Christian religion. Subsequently, the new colonial countries were established with the cultural religion of Christianity. Today, the overwhelming majority of so-called Western countries are by religious definition Christian—that is, Churchianity.

Chapter 5

Introduction

The 15 verses of chapter 5 shine a glorious and bright light for Israel's future and the future of the world. There is renewal for Israel and vengeance, anger, and fury "upon the heathen."

"The Judge of Israel"

Micah 5:1: "Now gather thyself in troops, O daughter of troops: he hath laid siege against us: they shall smite the judge of Israel with a rod upon the cheek."

(See) Job 16:10; Lamentations 3:30; Matthew 27:30

Who is this "judge of Israel?" Isaiah 53 identifies him, "...We did esteem him stricken, smitten of God, and afflicted. But he was wounded for our transgressions, he was bruised for our iniquities: the chastisement of our peace was upon him; and with his stripes we are healed" (verses 4-5). We read the fulfillment in Matthew 26:67: "Then did they spit in his face, and buffeted him; and others smote him with the palms of their hands."

Barnes Commentary explains: "'Others smote him with the palms of their hands' —the word used in the original here means literally to strike with rods."

It seems clear therefore that "the judge of Israel" is the Lord Jesus Christ. It was the Lord Himself who stated:

"For the Father judgeth no man, but hath committed all judgment unto the Son" (John 5:22).

"Daughter of Troops"

We must also emphasize that this verse is directed to the "daughter of troops," not to the mighty men of valor. It depicts Israel's condition during the time of the Messiah's appearance. Here we must read the statement Jesus made, "...Daughters of Jerusalem, weep not for me, but weep for yourselves, and for your children" (Luke 23:28). Jesus was prophesying what would happen to Jerusalem, and it was fulfilled in 70 A.D. What will happen at the end? "Then shall they begin to say to the mountains, Fall on us; and to the hills, Cover us" (Luke 23:30). These words go beyond two millennia of grace into the time of the Great Tribulation. We read of the fulfillment in Revelation 6:16, "And said to the mountains and rocks, Fall on us, and hide us from the face of him that sitteth on the throne, and from the wrath of the Lamb." This covers a time span between the first and the second coming of Jesus.

The Messiah's Birthplace

Micah 5:2: "But thou, Bethlehem Ephratah, though thou be little among the thousands of Judah, yet out of thee shall he come forth unto me that is to be ruler in Israel; whose goings forth have been from of old, from everlasting."

(See) Genesis 35:19; 49:10; Psalm 90:2; 132:6; Proverbs 8:22; Isaiah 9:6; Matthew 2:6; John 7:42

This is a clearly defined prophecy regarding the geographical location of the birth of Christ, "Bethlehem Ephratah." Again, there should be no second-guessing because there is only one "ruler in Israel; whose goings forth have been from of old, from everlasting."

Isaiah identifies this to be none other than Jesus Christ: "...His name shall be called Wonderful, Counsellor, The mighty God, The everlasting Father, The Prince of Peace" (Isaiah 9:6). This is also a clear documentation of the Holy Trinity. The Father, the Son and the Holy Spirit—Wonderful Counselor.

Return to Zion

Micah 5:3: "Therefore will he give them up, until the time that she which travaileth hath brought forth: then the remnant of his brethren shall return unto the children of Israel."

(See) Isaiah 10:20-22; Hosea 11:8

This verse is a reference to the regathering of the children of Israel. They were given up on; they experienced hopelessness without end and were persecuted the world over, fleeing from one place to another. Finally, they returned to Israel—the place from which they were cast out.

Yet God's intention is clearly recorded by the prophets: He wants to dwell in Zion, "Thus saith the LORD; I am returned unto Zion, and will dwell in the midst of Jerusalem: and Jerusalem shall be called a city of truth;

and the mountain of the LORD of hosts the holy mountain" (Zechariah 8:3). In order for Him to dwell in Zion,
His people, the Jews, must be present in the land of Israel. We read: "Thus saith the LORD of hosts; Behold, I
will save my people from the east country, and from the
west country; And I will bring them, and they shall dwell
in the midst of Jerusalem: and they shall be my people,
and I will be their God, in truth and in righteousness"
(verses 7-8). The first part is in fulfillment today, and the
second part, "I will be their God," is yet to be fulfilled.

The return of the children of Israel will lead to the return of the Messiah, and that will have a global effect:

Micah 5:4: "And he shall stand and feed in the strength of
the LORD, in the majesty of the name of the LORD his
God; and they shall abide: for now shall he be great unto
the ends of the earth."

(See) Psalm 72:8; Isaiah 52:13; Zechariah 9:10; Luke 1:32

This prophecy extends to our time, even into the millennium, the 1,000-year Kingdom of Peace. Jesus Christ is
not accepted at this point in time; that is, He is not
"great" in the eyes of the majority of people on earth,
but that will change. Isaiah proclaims, "I have sworn by
myself, the word is gone out of my mouth in righteousness, and shall not return, That unto me every knee shall
bow, every tongue shall swear" (Isaiah 45:23).

The Assyrian Connection

Micah 5:5-6: "And this man shall be the peace, when the Assyrian shall come into our land: and when he shall tread in our palaces, then shall we raise against him seven shepherds, and eight principal men. 6 And they shall waste the land of Assyria with the sword, and the land of Nimrod in the entrances thereof: thus shall he deliver us from the Assyrian, when he cometh into our land, and when he treadeth within our borders."

(See) Genesis 10:8; Isaiah 14:25; Zephaniah 2:13; Luke 1:71; 2:14

Who is this man of peace? He is the Word of God from eternity. Based on my understanding, this statement belongs with the previous verse.

Who are the "seven shepherds" and the eight "principal men"? There are diverse opinions among Bible scholars about their identity. However, we can with assurance say that the number seven represents completion. God rested on the seventh day of the creation week. Revelation 10:7 reads, "...In the days of the voice of the seventh angel, when he shall begin to sound, the mystery of God should be finished...." Eight indicates the new birth, the new day, the new creation.

Global Dispersion of the Jews

Micah 5:7: "And the remnant of Jacob shall be in the midst of many people as a dew from the LORD, as the showers upon the grass, that tarrieth not for man, nor waiteth for

274

the sons of men."

(See) Deuteronomy 32:2; Psalm 72:6; 110:3; Isaiah 44:3; Hosea 14:5

Note the positive aspect; they are a blessing: "...as a dew from the LORD, as the showers upon the grass." History records the many contributions Jews made to modern civilization, be it science, the arts, medicine, or music. There are no other people on earth who have put forth more brilliancy than the Jews. Note, however, the source is the LORD, and that blessing is independent of "the sons of men."

Judgment and Jews

Micah 5:8-9: "And the remnant of Jacob shall be among the Gentiles in the midst of many people as a lion among the beasts of the forest, as a young lion among the flocks of sheep: who, if he go through, both treadeth down, and teareth in pieces, and none can deliver. 9 Thine hand shall be lifted up upon thine adversaries, and all thine enemies shall be cut off."

(See) Genesis 49:9; Numbers 24:9; Psalm 10:12; 21:8; 44:5; Isaiah 26:11;
Hosea 5:14

This type of judgment may not be easily recognized, but judgment, as expressed in the Ten Commandments, comes from Israel. Every nation must obey the ten fundamental principles in order to maintain a functioning society.

Take a closer look at certain Jews in history: Karl Marx, the father of communism; Albert Einstein, the father of the nuclear bomb. Indeed, judgment is of the Jew, but so is salvation; it originates with the Jew.

"Wrath of the Lamb"

Let's consider an example in Revelation 6. Supernatural catastrophes will come upon the earth after the sixth seal has been opened. As a result, "And the kings of the earth, and the great men, and the rich men, and the chief captains, and the mighty men, and every bondman, and every free man, hid themselves in the dens and in the rocks of the mountains; And said to the mountains and rocks, Fall on us, and hide us from the face of him that sitteth on the throne, and from the wrath of the Lamb" (verses 15-16). Here we see the other side of the Lamb of God; *the wrath of the Lamb*. Believers know Him as "the Lamb of God, which taketh away the sin of the world." Unbelievers will experience "the wrath of the Lamb."

Separation from Idolatry

Micah 5:10-14: "And it shall come to pass in that day, saith the LORD, that I will cut off thy horses out of the midst of thee, and I will destroy thy chariots: 11 And I will cut off the cities of thy land, and throw down all thy strong holds: 12 And I will cut off witchcrafts out of thine hand; and thou shalt have no more soothsayers: 13 Thy graven images also will I cut off, and thy standing images out of the midst of thee; and thou shalt no more worship the work of thine hands. 14 And I will pluck up thy groves out of the midst of thee: so will I destroy thy cities."

(See) Isaiah 2:8, 18; 17:8; 27:9; Hosea 14:3; Zechariah 9:10; 13:2

After returning from Babylonian captivity, the Jews were healed from "graven images." Until this day, they "no more worship the work of [their] hands."

This progressive judgment, which will climax in the Great Tribulation and finally the Battle of Armageddon, will affect the entire world:

Micah 5:15: "And I will execute vengeance in anger and fury upon the heathen, such as they have not heard."

This is vengeance against "the heathen," not Jacob. Jeremiah states, "Alas! for that day is great, so that none is like it: it is even the time of Jacob's trouble; but he shall be saved out of it" (Jeremiah 30:7).

Chapter 6

Introduction

If we ask why the prophet addressed the mountains, the hills and the foundations of the earth, then we must note that the geographical and topographical earth is subject to God: He is the Creator of the entire universe. Thus, the earth too is subject to radical renewal. We read Romans 8:22 in this connection: "For we know that the whole creation groaneth and travaileth in pain together until now."

The extent to which planet Earth participates in God's plan of salvation is evident from the events that transpired when Jesus, the eternal Son of God, died on Calvary's cross: "And, behold, the veil of the temple was rent in twain from the top to the bottom; and the earth did quake, and the rocks rent" (Matthew 27:51). We have a record that the universe was involved even before that event took place: "Now from the sixth hour there was darkness over all the land unto the ninth hour" (verse 45). Yes, God does speak to the earth: it is His creation.

The prophet Ezekiel had to speak to the geographical, topical land of Israel: "Also, thou son of man, prophesy unto the mountains of Israel, and say, Ye mountains of Israel, hear the word of the LORD" (Ezekiel 36:1). The land had to be prepared for the people, which is confirmed in verse 8: "But ye, O mountains of Israel, ye shall shoot forth your branches, and yield your fruit to my

278

people of Israel; for they are at hand to come."

The Lord's Controversy

Micah 6:1-2: "Hear ye now what the LORD saith; Arise, contend thou before the mountains, and let the hills hear thy voice. 2 Hear ye, O mountains, the Lord's controversy, and ye strong foundations of the earth: for the Lord hath a controversy with his people, and he will plead with Israel."

(See) 2 Samuel 22:16; Psalm 104:5; Hosea 4:1

There should be no question that the mountains, hills, and foundation of the earth are able to hear the voice of God. After all, God spoke all of creation into existence. When God speaks, His creation listens.

God reveals the controversy He has with His people with simple questions:

Micah 6:3-4: "O my people, what have I done unto thee? and wherein have I wearied thee? testify against me. 4 For I brought thee up out of the land of Egypt, and redeemed thee out of the house of servants; and I sent before thee Moses, Aaron, and Miriam."

(See) Psalm 50:7; Isaiah 5:3-4; Jeremiah 2:5, 31

Israel collectively accused God with their works, their behavior, and their actions. They should have remembered their redemption from slavery in Egypt and understood that the God of creation had good intentions for them, but they stubbornly refused to heed the Word of God.

The incident of Balaam and Balak is cited as an accusation against Israel:

Micah 6:5: "O my people, remember now what Balak king of Moab consulted, and what Balaam the son of Beor answered him from Shittim unto Gilgal; that ye may know the righteousness of the LORD."

(See) Numbers 22:5; 25:1; Judges 5:11; Revelation 2:14

Balaam's Prophecy

The prophet even quotes an important event in Israel's early history, when Balaam the prophet made this statement about Israel: "He hath not beheld iniquity in Jacob, neither hath he seen perverseness in Israel: the LORD his God is with him, and the shout of a king is among them. God brought them out of Egypt; he hath as it were the strength of an unicorn. Surely there is no enchantment against Jacob, neither is there any divination against Israel: according to this time it shall be said of Jacob and of Israel, What hath God wrought!" (Numbers 23:21-23).

Bible readers are familiar with Israel's behavior and how they repeatedly rebelled against Moses and the Lord God. Actually, there was not much good to report about Israel. Yet here we learn as Gentiles to view Israel from God's perspective, not from ours: no iniquity, no perverseness, no enchantment, no divination—that is God's

280

Israel. That is "what God has wrought!"

What a lesson to learn. We have no right to judge, much less condemn, our fellow man, particularly Christians who do not think, act or believe according to our understanding. Every Christian, born again of the Spirit of God, is a miracle: "what God has wrought!"

Four Questions

Micah 6:6-7: "Wherewith shall I come before the LORD, and bow myself before the high God? shall I come before him with burnt offerings, with calves of a year old? 7 Will the LORD be pleased with thousands of rams, or with ten thousands of rivers of oil? shall I give my first-born for my transgression, the fruit of my body for the sin of my soul?"

(See) 2 Kings 16:3; Psalm 15:1; 50:9; Isaiah 1:11; John 6:28

These four questions expose the people's hopelessness to reconcile themselves in relationship to the controversy the Lord God had with His people. In other words, the prophet asked four questions which were categorically answered with "no." The controversy could not be solved with man's ability to humble himself, nor could he solve it by sacrificing all that he had—in this case, livestock and produce. Even the thought of giving one's "firstborn for my transgression" could not atone for his sin and thereby solve the controversy.

But this last question has prophetic content, because it reveals God's thoughts and His intention to not only

281

solve the controversy with Israel, but also with mankind. We read the answer in one of the most popular Bible verses: "For God so loved the world, that he gave his only begotten Son, that whosoever believeth in him should not perish, but have everlasting life" (John 3:16).

None of our own actions can atone for the irreparable damage that was caused by our transgressions, nor can we solve God's controversy with His people. But here is what they and we must do:

> **Micah 6:8:** "He hath showed thee, O man, what is good; and what doth the LORD require of thee, but to do justly, and to love mercy, and to walk humbly with thy God?"

> (See) Deuteronomy 10:12; Isaiah 56:1; Jeremiah 22:3

This verse reveals man's responsibility toward God. It exposes the contrast we read in the previous verses, which showed that no matter how hard we may try, we are incapable of reconciling ourselves to God.

Salvation in His Word

> **Micah 6:9:** "The LORD'S voice crieth unto the city, and the man of wisdom shall see thy name: hear ye the rod, and who hath appointed it."

The Menge translation is helpful in this instance: "Hearken, the Lord calleth the city, and wise is he who learns to fear his name. Take notice of the rod of correction and

Him who hath ordered it." In other words, hear and heed the Word of God. There is salvation only in Him!

> **Micah 6:10-12:** "Are there yet the treasures of wickedness in the house of the wicked, and the scant measure that is abominable? 11 Shall I count them pure with the wicked balances, and with the bag of deceitful weights? 12 For the rich men thereof are full of violence, and the inhabitants thereof have spoken lies, and their tongue is deceitful in their mouth."
>
> (See) Isaiah 1:23; Jeremiah 5:26-27; 9:8; Ezekiel 45:9-10; Hosea 12:7; Amos 3:10; 8:5

How did Israel react to God's revealed plan of salvation? They treated it with total disregard. God's righteousness was violated by the acts of the people: "Treasures of wickedness...scant measure...abominable...wicked balances...deceitful weights...violence...spoken lies...deceitful...mouth." God cannot forgive unconditionally; that would violate His righteousness. Someone had to pay for sin committed. "The soul that sinneth, it shall die"—that is irreversible. But God had a plan: in due time Jesus, the sinless One, came and paid in full the penalty for sin, once and for all.

No Righteousness in the World

We must not view this solely as a historical fact or as a prophetic pronouncement against Israel in the future, but accept it for our time too. Someone may object and say, "We do no such thing. We are law-abiding citizens. We do the right thing." If you have any doubt about man's basic inability to act righteously, just open your local directory and look at all the listings under the heading "Attorneys." In a dishonest, corrupt and unrighteous society, we need interpreters of the law. Why? Because we do not accept truth that stands in opposition to our opinion. Those who deal with the law will never be unemployed until the Righteous One comes and the law is proclaimed to the world from Zion.

Now God declares what He will do in response to Israel's stubborn refusal to repent, turn away from evil, and heed the Word of God.

Israel's Failure

Micah 6:13-15: "Therefore also will I make thee sick in smiting thee, in making thee desolate because of thy sins. 14 Thou shalt eat, but not be satisfied; and thy casting down shall be in the midst of thee; and thou shalt take hold, but shalt not deliver; and that which thou deliverest will I give up to the sword. 15 Thou shalt sow, but thou shalt not reap; thou shalt tread the olives, but thou shalt not anoint thee with oil; and sweet wine, but shalt not drink wine."

(See) Deuteronomy 28:38-40; Isaiah 1:7; 6:11; 9:20; Amos 5:11;
Zephaniah 1:13

This is a curse upon the work, the hope and the aspiration of the people God had chosen. They deliberately chose to disobey His instruction. Had Israel followed

God's words, the harvest of the land would be in abundance.

Reason for God's Controversy

Micah 6:16: "For the statutes of Omri are kept, and all the works of the house of Ahab, and ye walk in their counsels; that I should make thee a desolation, and the inhabitants thereof an hissing: therefore ye shall bear the reproach of my people."

(See) 1 Kings 16:25-26, 29-33; Psalm 44:13; Jeremiah 7:24; 18:16; 19:8

Instead of Israel following Judah, Judah is following Israel. Omri was the son of Ahab, king of Israel, and there is little doubt that these two kings were the most wicked. As a result, Israel was led into captivity, the land became desolate, and the remnant became a mockery and a reproach to all the people who passed by.

Prophecy of Moses Fulfilled

What Moses had prophesied did in fact come to pass: "And thou shalt become an astonishment, a proverb, and a byword, among all nations whither the LORD shall lead thee. Thou shalt carry much seed out into the field, and shalt gather but little in; for the locust shall consume it. Thou shalt plant vineyards, and dress them, but shalt neither drink of the wine, nor gather the grapes; for the worms shall eat them. Thou shalt have olive trees throughout all thy coasts, but thou shalt not anoint thyself with the oil; for thine olive shall cast his fruit. Thou

285

shalt beget sons and daughters, but thou shalt not enjoy them; for they shall go into captivity. All thy trees and fruit of thy land shall the locust consume. The stranger that is within thee shall get up above thee very high; and thou shalt come down very low" (Deuteronomy 28:37-43).

History documents the many horrible judgments that had befallen the Jews. Some historians claim that over 14 million Jews have been killed since the destruction of the temple in Jerusalem in 70 A.D. Even in the last century, more than six million Jews were systematically slaughtered under Adolf Hitler and his Nazi regime.

Prophecy has been fulfilled in the past, is being fulfilled today, and will be fulfilled in the future—in accordance with the written Word of God!

Chapter 7

Introduction

The first six verses of this last chapter are a prophecy of darkness. But then, there is hope in the midst of chaos and confusion; this hope is expressed with the words, "I will wait for the God of my salvation." God's action, based on His compassion for His people, concludes the book of Micah.

From Hopelessness to Glorious Hope

Micah 7:1: "Woe is me! for I am as when they have gathered the summer fruits, as the grapegleanings of the vintage: there is no cluster to eat: my soul desired the firstripe fruit."

(See) Isaiah 24:13; 28:4; Jeremiah 2:3; Hosea 9:10

Micah was a prophet of God who had to proclaim a very difficult message to the people. But he also was a *priest* in the sense that he identified himself with the sins of his people: "Woe is me!" He doesn't say, "Woe unto Israel, Judah, or Jerusalem," but very personally, "me."

Furthermore, he identifies himself with the "grapegleanings" and the desire for the "first-ripe fruit." In plain words, he is saying: "My situation is hopeless. The summer fruits are gone, and there is nothing left, not even the gleanings." Talk about hopelessness; this cer-

287

tainly is a horrible picture the Holy Spirit passes on to His people and to us through the prophet Micah.

Not Gentiles but Israel

There are a number of excellent Bible scholars who attempt to spiritualize the matter and transfer the message of judgment to their own country. When we follow that line, we are aiming in the wrong direction. Whether it is the United States or any other country in the world, it cannot and must not be compared with the land and people of Israel.

One scholar came to the conclusion, "Judgment was pronounced upon Israel because of their sin. Judgment did come, and so will judgment come upon America because of her sin." It may sound biblical, but it is false in principle. The laws, statutes, and commandments God gave were directed exclusively to the people of Israel and to no other nation in the world. The God of Israel, the Creator of heaven and earth, specifically and emphatically addresses His Word to the people who came "out of Egypt." This phrase appears about 200 times throughout Scripture. This has no relationship to any political identity from among the Gentile nations of the world—it never has and never will.

Never Compare Israel with Gentiles

We can be as proud as we want; as fanatical, nationalistic and patriotic as we can be. We can jump up and down, waving our flags dozens of times and shouting, "God bless America!" until we are blue in the face. Yet it is nothing more than pagan blabber. We cannot detour the clearly documented words of the Bible, such as Isaiah 40:17: "All nations before him are as nothing; and they are counted to him less than nothing, and vanity."

Nevertheless, we from among the Gentiles, who are born into the family of God through the rebirth, are a different identity. Ephesians 2:12 reads, "That at that time ye were without Christ, being aliens from the commonwealth of Israel, and strangers from the covenants of promise, having no hope, and without God in the world." Thus, all nations in the world fall under the category of "no hope." Yet, the individual members from among the nations, who have placed their faith in Jesus Christ the Lord, are distinctly different, "But now in Christ Jesus ye who sometimes were far off are made nigh by the blood of Christ...Now therefore ye are no more strangers and foreigners, but fellowcitizens with the saints, and of the household of God" (Ephesians 2:13, 19). We have now become heavenly citizens. The Church is a special, God-ordained entity, independent of any nation.

The Rapture?

Micah 7:2: "The good man is perished out of the earth: and there is none upright among men: they all lie in wait for blood; they hunt every man his brother with a net."

(See) Isaiah 57:1; 59:7; Jeremiah 5:26; Hosea 5:1

What happened to "the good man"? In Micah's case, we must presume they had died; they went to their spiritual home. It says, "perished out of the earth." Doubtless, this is also a prophecy of the Church of Jesus Christ. Suddenly, unannounced and in the twinkling of an eye, the Church will be "out of the earth." Then "the good man" will be gone.

Even the Best Are No Good

Micah goes on to expose the morally, politically, judicially and economically corrupt system:

> **Micah 7:3-4:** "That they may do evil with both hands earnestly, the prince asketh, and the judge asketh for a reward; and the great man, he uttereth his mischievous desire: so they wrap it up. 4 The best of them is as a brier: the most upright is sharper than a thorn hedge: the day of thy watchmen and thy visitation cometh; now shall be their perplexity."

(See) Proverbs 4:16-17; Isaiah 1:23; 10:3; 22:5; Hosea 9:7; Amos 5:12;
Nahum 1:10

Micah reveals something that is not obvious; it was not made visible. At that time, the political identity was still intact, so there is a prince, a judge, and there are great men. Notice, however, that their motive in life is totally saturated by the Luciferian spirit. This is expressed with the word "asketh." What are they asking for? Bribes and profit; that is, "mischievous desire."

Technological Control Replaces Spirit Control

In today's world, a judge better not ask for a reward, nor

a politician for benefits. Why not? Have the people become better today than they used to be in olden days? The answer is rather simple: no! But, they can no longer get away with it (for the most part). We have entered the dispensation of technological control. Almost daily we read and hear reports from the international media, where government officials, men and women in high positions, are being caught violating the law. This is primarily due to technology. When more control is implemented, less corruption will be the result. Total control of all movement in government, finance, business and religion—not to mention private citizens—is only a matter of time.

People, regardless of their level of sophistication or education, do not become better people; they are just as corrupt and sinful as ever. The words God spoke about the pre-Flood people are applicable to today as well: "And God looked upon the earth, and, behold, it was corrupt; for all flesh had corrupted his way upon the earth" (Genesis 6:12).

However, the fact that crime, violence, and brutality have significantly decreased can be documented by reliable statistics the world over. That leads many to the conclusion that the world is getting better; people are more honest; we are approaching a peaceful global society. Are we, really? The answer is NO. The seeming contradiction is explained by today's technological control.

Church Morals

Speaking of the Church, it will be worse in the end stages of the end times. "This know also, that in the last days perilous times shall come. For men shall be lovers of their own selves, covetous, boasters, proud, blasphemers, disobedient to parents, unthankful, unholy, Without natural affection, trucebreakers, false accusers, incontinent, fierce, despisers of those that are good, Traitors, heady, highminded, lovers of pleasures more than lovers of God; Having a form of godliness, but denying the power thereof: from such turn away" (2 Timothy 3:1-5).

"In the last days perilous times shall come." God judges the world from different perspectives than we ourselves may judge it. However, we must point out that these "perilous times" will be found and experienced in the Church.

It is our belief that the world indeed will see less crime, corruption, brutality and war in the future, but not because man is getting more refined; the truth is, better control is being implemented.

Stealing cash, for example, as an employee in a retail store, has become virtually impossible. All merchandise is barcoded, all payments are registered, and at the end of the day, the person responsible for the cash register must give account.

Israel's Moral Bankruptcy

In Israel's case, it was hopeless because even "the best of them is as a brier." Luther translates "brier" with the word "thorns." Here we are reminded of the curse: "Thorns also and thistles shall it bring forth to thee; and thou shalt eat the herb of the field" (Genesis 3:18).

End Time Realities

Micah 7:5-6: "Trust ye not in a friend, put ye not confidence in a guide: keep the doors of thy mouth from her that lieth in thy bosom. 6 For the son dishonoureth the father, the daughter riseth up against her mother, the daughter in law against her mother in law; a man's enemies are the men of his own house."

(See) Genesis 9:22, 24; Jeremiah 9:4; Matthew 10:21, 35-36; Luke 12:53

This indeed is a strong statement; in other words, be cautious what you say to your friend, your children, yes, even your spouse. We are living in the digital age; no one really knows what is being recorded electronically. We have to keep in mind that the epitome of total control will be exercised by the false prophet, who endorses, supports, and propagandizes the beast, the Antichrist, "And he had power to give life unto the image of the beast, that the image of the beast should both speak, and cause that as many as would not worship the image of the beast should be killed" (Revelation 13:15).

How does this manmade image distinguish between those who worship and those who do not worship? Computer technology will make it possible. At this point in time, scientists are developing computers that can read your mind. Total law and total control will ultimately be implemented.

Surely, the prophet also speaks of the time of the Church. Jesus had this to say: "For I am come to set a man at variance against his father, and the daughter against her mother, and the daughter in law against her mother in law. And a man's foes shall be they of his own household" (Matthew 10:35-36). This is nothing other than total separation from the things of the world in order to follow Christ Jesus. Does that mean we no longer honor our family, or disrespect our father and mother? Not at all, for the Bible says, "Honour thy father and mother; (which is the first commandment with promise)" (Ephesians 6:2).

Yet Jesus said, "If any man come to me, and hate not his father, and mother, and wife, and children, and brethren, and sisters, yea, and his own life also, he cannot be my disciple" (Luke 14:26). Note it says, "and his own life also." In plain words, everything of significance here on earth while in our flesh and blood, becomes insignificant in relationship to following the Lord Jesus Christ.

Wait for the Lord

Micah 7:7: "Therefore I will look unto the LORD; I will wait for the God of my salvation: my God will hear me."

(See) Psalm 4:3; 130:5; Isaiah 25:9; Habakkuk 2:1

These words struck me because of the prophet's precise and determined expression of his dependence upon God. Doubtless, he was deeply moved by this experience, and while he uttered and wrote down these words, he was trembling before the living God. But he knew with absolute certainty that "God will hear me."

We need to learn from this because prophecy in general is considered to be something that is difficult to understand, and there are innumerable interpretations of various events. Subsequently, scholars have specialized in proclaiming the sensational aspects of prophecy. As a result, many dear Christians buy books, subscribe to magazines and attend prophecy conferences, assuming they can gain from the presentation without being personally involved. They will be disappointed. Prophecy is part of the Bible. We "are built upon the foundation of the apostles and prophets, Jesus Christ himself being the chief cornerstone" (Ephesians 2:20). Prophecy is something very personal; it draws you away from the things of the world to the things which are yet invisible. The moment I am confronted in my spirit with the invisible realities, I no longer seek sensationalism, but my target is "Jesus Christ, and him crucified" (1 Corinthians 2:2).

Whenever I am involved personally, I immediately recognize my own wretchedness, my inability to comprehend the depths of God. Prophecy teaches me to recognize my total and absolute dependence upon His grace.

The prophet Micah shows both sides of the coin; those who are against him, the enemies, and his reliance on God's immeasurable grace.

Restoring Grace

Micah 7:8-10: "Rejoice not against me, O mine enemy: when I fall, I shall arise; when I sit in darkness, the LORD shall be a light unto me. 9 I will bear the indignation of the LORD, because I have sinned against him, until he plead my cause, and execute judgment for me: he will bring me forth to the light, and I shall behold his righteousness. 10 Then she that is mine enemy shall see it, and shame shall cover her which said unto me, Where is the LORD thy God? mine eyes shall behold her: now shall she be trodden down as the mire of the streets."

(See) Psalm 37:5-6; Proverbs 24:17; Isaiah 9:2; 46:13; 56:1; Lamentations 4:21; Joel 2:17; Obadiah 12; Zechariah 10:5

The revelation of the Victor will take place—that's a given: "Behold, he cometh with clouds; and every eye shall see him, and they also which pierced him: and all kindreds of the earth shall wail because of him. Even so, Amen" (Revelation 1:7). Apparently, no rejoicing; no glorious future for the rest of the world. There is no hope without Jesus Christ our Lord.

Promise of Restoration

Micah 7:11-13: "In the day that thy walls are to be built, in that day shall the decree be far removed. 12 In that day also he shall come even to thee from Assyria, and from the fortified cities, and from the fortress even to the river, and from sea to sea, and from mountain to mountain. 13 Notwithstanding the land shall be desolate because of them that dwell therein, for the fruit of their doings."

(See) Isaiah 19:23-25; Jeremiah 25:11; Amos 9:11

The pronunciation of judgment upon Israel continues. To better understand these three verses, let us read them in the *Tenakh*, "A day for mending your walls—That is a far-off day. This is rather a day when to you [Tramplers] will come streaming from Assyria and the towns of Egypt—From [every land from] Egypt to the Euphrates, from sea to sea and from mountain to mountain—And your land shall become a desolation—Because of those who dwell in it—as the fruit of their misdeeds." This is a prophecy relating to Israel's return, "A day for mending your walls." Israel has been busy since 1948 rebuilding their walls, but the enemies do not rest.

It is of interest that the *Tenakh* names the river, the Euphrates. That is the northern border of the Promised Land, and the river of Egypt is the southern border. It is my understanding that the desolation, the destruction of the land of Israel found its fulfillment during the last 2,000 years, but Israel is now in the beginning stages of renewal.

"Feed Thy People"

Micah 7:14-15: "Feed thy people with thy rod, the flock of thine heritage, which dwell solitarily in the wood, in the midst of Carmel: let them feed in Bashan and Gilead, as in the days of old. 15 According to the days of thy coming out of the land of Egypt will I show unto him marvellous things."

(See) Exodus 3:20; 34:10; Numbers 23:9; Deuteronomy 33:28; Psalm 78:12; Jeremiah 50:19

The restoring of Israel is a reality in our days, but it's not the end; rather, the beginning. The enemies cannot say anything against it, though they have spoken negatively, acted brutally, and threatened Israel with destruction. When God deals with His people openly, truth is manifested. They can only be silent.

Micah 7:16-17: "The nations shall see and be confounded at all their might: they shall lay their hand upon their mouth, their ears shall be deaf. 17 They shall lick the dust like a serpent, they shall move out of their holes like worms of the earth: they shall be afraid of the LORD our God, and shall fear because of thee."

(See) Deuteronomy 32:24; Isaiah 25:3; 26:11; 49:23; 59:19

In the end, what was written by the prophet Isaiah, a contemporary of Micah, will come to pass, "I have sworn by myself, the word is gone out of my mouth in righteousness, and shall not return, That unto me every knee shall bow, every tongue shall swear" (Isaiah 45:23).

"The Truth to Jacob, and the Mercy to Abraham"

Finally, the prophet joyfully proclaims the inexhaustible grace of the God of Israel:

Micah 7:18-20: "Who is a God like unto thee, that pardoneth iniquity, and passeth by the transgression of the remnant of his heritage? he retaineth not his anger for

298

ever, because he delighteth in mercy. 19 He will turn again, he will have compassion upon us; he will subdue our iniquities; and thou wilt cast all their sins into the depths of the sea. 20 Thou wilt perform the truth to Jacob, and the mercy to Abraham, which thou hast sworn unto our fathers from the days of old."

(See) Exodus 15:11; 34:6-7; Deuteronomy 7:8-12;
Psalm 89:6, 8; 103:8-9, 13; Isaiah 57:16

Why "the truth to Jacob, and the mercy to Abraham"? The truth about Jacob lies in his change of name from Jacob, "deceiver" to Israel, "fighter of God." And Abraham, who is called the father of all believers, is the recipient of grace.

There is no other way outside the grace of God to be pardoned, forgiven and restored.

God's Act of Grace

The prophet Micah thundered his message of judgment against God's people. They had fallen away from God, dealt corruptly and stubbornly with Him and His law, but now He proclaims restoration. What is the reason? Not because of their deeds; not because of anything they deserved. Not even because of Micah, but because God loves His people. He has found a way to satisfy His righteousness; namely, the blood of His beloved Son, the Lord Jesus Christ, who paid in full for the sins, not only of Israel, but also for all of mankind.

Take Hold of Grace

Today is still the day of grace: anyone who wishes to receive unconditional forgiveness may obtain it by asking, and it's FREE. For about 2,000 years, the message has continued to be proclaimed: "And it shall come to pass, that whosoever shall call on the name of the Lord shall be saved" (Acts 2:21). But be cautious, for there is no alternative: either your sins are paid for once and for all, or your guilt will remain with you forever. John 3:36 makes this clear: "He that believeth on the Son hath everlasting life: and he that believeth not the Son shall not see life; but the wrath of God abideth on him."

NOTES

NOTES

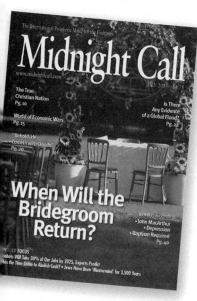